STUDENT ACTIVITIES WORKBOOK

Mc
Graw
Hill
Education

MHEonline.com

Copyright © McGraw-Hill Education

All rights reserved. No part of this publication may be
reproduced or distributed in any form or by any means, or
stored in a database or retrieval system, without the
prior written consent of McGraw-Hill Education,
including, but not limited to, network storage or
transmission, or broadcast for distance learning.

Send all inquiries to:
McGraw-Hill Education
8787 Orion Place
Columbus, OH 43240

ISBN: 978-0-07-875062-5
MHID: 0-07-875062-8

Printed in the United States of America.

11 12 13 14 15 16 17 18 19 RHR 20 19 18 17 16

Table of Contents

Introduction

This Workbook contains Study Guides, Activities, Health Inventories, and Applying Health Skills activities to accompany the chapters in your student textbook.

The Study Guides are to be completed as you read each lesson. They will help you check your understanding of lesson content. Each Study Guide consists of questions to help you outline the main ideas in the chapter. After you have completed all the questions, you can use the Study Guide to review the information in the chapter as a whole.

Following each Study Guide, there are Activities—one for each lesson in your textbook. The Activities give you opportunities to apply what you have learned. A variety of formats is offered, including fill-ins, short-answer, matching, classifying, and sequencing. In some Activities, you are asked to complete or analyze a chart, or to label a diagram.

A Health Inventory follows the Activities for each *odd* chapter. Each Health Inventory offers you an opportunity to assess your own health or health behaviors. The purpose of the Health Inventories is to help you recognize what you are doing that is good for your health and identify behaviors that you need to change.

An Applying Health Skills activity follows the Activities for each *even* chapter. Each Health Skills activity gives you an opportunity to practice one of the ten health skills introduced in Chapter 1 of your textbook. These skills can help you stay healthy throughout your entire life.

Chapter 1 Study Guide
Understanding Your Health

Study Tips
✔ Read the chapter objectives.
✔ Look up any unfamiliar words.
✔ Read the questions below before you read the chapter.

As you read the chapter, answer the following questions. Later you can use this guide to review the information in the chapter.

Lesson 1

1. What does it mean to be healthy?

_____

_____

2. Name the three parts of the health triangle, and list two aspects of each side.

_____

_____

_____

_____

_____

_____

_____

_____

3. Why is it important to keep your health triangle balanced?

_____

_____

4. Explain why wellness is more than just being healthy.

_____

_____

_____

Chapter 1 Study Guide
Understanding Your Health

Chapter 1

Lesson 2

5. Identify three characteristics of adolescence.

_____

_____

_____

_____

6. What are *hormones?*

_____

_____

7. List two changes that occur during adolescence for each of the following: physical growth, mental and emotional growth, and social growth.

_____

_____

_____

_____

_____

_____

_____

_____

_____

8. Define *community service.*

_____

_____

Chapter 1 Study Guide
Understanding Your Health

Lesson 3

9. What are lifestyle factors?

_____

_____

10. Identify three examples of positive lifestyle factors.

_____

_____

_____

_____

_____

11. Explain why a sendentary lifestyle is a risk behavior.

_____

_____

_____

12. Explain why abstinence from risk behaviors is a wise choice for teens.

_____

_____

_____

Activity 1
Use with Chapter 1, Lesson 1

The Signs of Good Health

Read the statements in the left column. If the statement describes good health, place a check next to it in the middle column. In the right column identify the type of health being described. Your choices are: physical health, mental/emotional health, and social health. Leave blank any statement that does not describe a sign of good health.

Descriptions		Type of Health
1. Tom has played both football and baseball for 5 years.		
2. Jane gets along well with others and makes friends easily.		
3. John feels as though he has many faults and constantly worries about his mistakes.		
4. To help him relax, Jordan has the habit of taking long walks daily.		
5. Fred smokes.		
6. Lisa gets regular check-ups from medical professionals.		
7. Ted handles stressful situations and challenges with a positive attitude.		
8. When Andy has problems, he is unable to find solutions.		
9. Shannon is negative and critical towards others.		
10. Meg keeps her thoughts to herself and rarely expresses what she feels.		
11. Tim values and respects others.		
12. Jamie makes friends quickly, but does not keep them. He spends most of his free time alone.		
13. Sam refuses to spend time with his family.		
14. Martin eats healthy meals and enjoys cooking.		
15. Each year Sean has intense conflict with at least three of his teachers.		

Activity 2
Use with Chapter 1, Lesson 2

Changes During the Teen Years

Read each question. Then, write the answer that you think a health professional would give.

Question	Answer from a health care professional
1. What makes me so different?	
2. Sometimes I want to stay a child. Why am I afraid to become an adult?	
3. Both of my best friends look like young women. Why do I still look like a little girl?	
4. Why do I feel so awkward, like my arms and legs do not belong to me any more?	
5. Sometimes I get so confused when I listen to people argue. I can see both points of view and cannot decide who is right.	
6. When I listen to people talk about politics, I find myself interested. I wonder why that is, since I never cared about politics before.	
7. Why do I feel happy one moment and sad the next?	
8. Why do I often think about what college I want to go to and what kind of job I want?	

Chapter 1

Activity 3
Use with Chapter 1, Lesson 3

Taking Responsibility for Your Health

   Imagine that you have been asked to create a display for the front hall in your school. The topic for the display is the positive consequences of following healthy behaviors.

The title for the display is, "Healthy Behaviors."

In each of the flags below, you have been directed to include:

   1. A healthy behavior

   2. The benefit of the healthy behavior.

The first one is done for you.

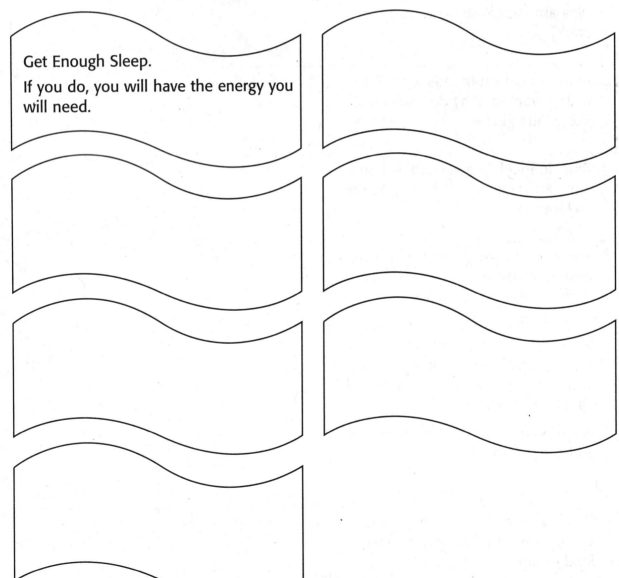

Get Enough Sleep.
If you do, you will have the energy you will need.

Chapter 1 Health Inventory

Your Total Health

Read the statements below. In the space at the left, write *yes* **if the statement describes you, or** *no* **if it does not describe you.**

_____ **1.** I accept constructive criticism when it is given.

_____ **2.** I feel comfortable when meeting new people.

_____ **3.** I get at least 8 hours of sleep a night.

_____ **4.** I eat a variety of healthy foods.

_____ **5.** I stay within 5 pounds of my appropriate weight range.

_____ **6.** I can accept other people's ideas and suggestions.

_____ **7.** I do 20 minutes or more of vigorous physical activity at least three times a week.

_____ **8.** I am happy most of the time.

_____ **9.** I can accept differences in people.

_____ **10.** I can say no to my friends if they are doing something I do not want to do.

_____ **11.** I have at least one or two close friends.

_____ **12.** I ask for help when I need it.

_____ **13.** I seldom feel tired or run-down.

_____ **14.** I can express my feelings to others in healthy ways.

_____ **15.** I can name at least three activities I perform well.

Score yourself:

Write the number of *yes* answers here. ☐

12–15: Your health practices are very good.

8–11: Your health practices are good.

5–7: Your health practices are fair.

Fewer than 5: Your health practices are in need of some changes.

Chapter 2 Study Guide
Skills for a Healthy Life

Study Tips
✔ Read the chapter objectives.
✔ Look up any unfamiliar words.
✔ Read the questions below before you read the chapter.

As you read the chapter, answer the following questions. Later you can use this guide to review the information in the chapter.

Lesson 1

1. Define *decision making* and explain the value of having decision-making skills.

_____

_____

2. What are the six steps in the decision-making process?

_____

_____

3. Define *goal setting,* and explain the benefit of goal-setting skills.

_____

_____

4. Name the six steps of the goal-setting process.

_____

_____

_____

_____

Lesson 2

5. Define *character.*

_____

_____

Chapter 2 Study Guide
Skills for a Healthy Life

6. What are the six main traits that work together to form good character?

_____

_____

7. Define *tolerance* and *prejudice*. Explain how the two words relate to each other.

_____

_____

_____

8. Give three examples of qualities found in caring people.

_____

_____

_____

_____

Lesson 3

9. Name the five health skills that relate to communication.

_____

_____

10. What does practicing healthful behaviors help you do?

_____

11. Define *stress*.

_____

_____

12. What are ways to manage stress?

_____

Activity 4
Use with Chapter 2, Lesson 1

Making Decisions and Setting Goals

Amber loves life and other people, but she feels like she makes one bad decision after another. She feels that sometimes her life lacks purpose even though she works hard and wants to do the right thing.

Read the following snapshot from Amber's life. After the snapshot, you will find charts of the steps for decision making and the steps of goal setting. Beside the steps on each chart, fill in what you think Amber should have done differently in the situation.

Snapshot of Amber

Amber is an outgoing, social teen. She loves to laugh and to have fun with others. Monday, during lunch, she announced that she is having a party that Friday night. All day people told her that they would come. Since she was not sure how many would attend her party, she ordered quantities of snacks and soda to be delivered on Friday morning. Then, she bought a new dress to wear. On Wednesday she spent the evening making up party games and activities. By Thursday she sat down with her mother to go over her party activities. Her mother was angry because her aunt and her six children were due to arrive Friday morning. Friday, Amber went to school in a bad mood because she had to tell everyone that the party was off.

The Decision-Making Process	What Amber should have done differently
Step 1: State the Situation	
Step 2: List the Options	
Step 3: Weigh the Possible Outcomes	
Step 4: Considering Your Values	
Step 5: Make a Decision and Act	
Step 6: Evaluate Your Decision	

Activity 4
Use with Chapter 2, Lesson 1

The Goal-Setting Process	What Amber should have done differently
Step 1: Identify a Specific Goal and Write It Down	
Step 2: List the Steps You Will Take to Reach Your Goal	
Step 3: Get Help and Support from Others	
Step 4: Identifying and Overcoming Specific Obstacles	
Step 5: Evaluate Your Progress	
Step 6: Give Yourself a Reward Once You Have Achieved Your Goal	

Activity 5
Use with Chapter 2, Lesson 2

Chapter 2

Building Good Character

At your school assembly this month, three people are being given "Good Character Awards." You are given the task of introducing each person. To prepare, you take notes about what each person has done to be given the "Good Character Award." In addition, you review the traits of good character that you learned in health class. They include: **trustworthiness, respect, responsibility, fairness, caring,** and **citizenship.**

Directions: Under the card with the notes about each person, write your introduction. Be sure to identify how the person's activities show the specific traits of good character.

1.

Fred

- Goes around the neighborhood collecting food and clothing for the local charities

- Gets cash sometimes, but never keeps any of it

- Takes turns going to all of the different charities around the area, so each charity gets its fair share

Your introduction of Fred:

2.

Mary

- Babysits for mothers in her neighborhood for an affordable fee

- Rocks infants, reads stories to toddlers, takes youngsters on nature walks

- Leaves the house clean with toys picked up

- Does not allow kids to break rules

Your introduction of Mary:

Activity 5
Use with Chapter 2, Lesson 2

3.

Cheryl
• Volunteers at an after-school program in an elementary school
• Plays games and reads to the children
• Helps others with homework
• Listens to problems, but never repeats what is said
• Makes sure all of the children get attention and concern

Your introduction of Cheryl:

Activity 6
Use with Chapter 2, Lesson 3

Developing Other Health Skills

Read the following statements that describe real-life situations. In the space on the left, write the health skill that could help solve the situation. On the line provided, write the question that should be asked to guide the situation.

Health Skills are:

Communication	Analyze Influences	Conflict Resolution	Advocacy
Access Information	Refusal Skills	Stress Management	

_____ 1. Cars speed up and down the streets by the school. These streets are used by children who walk home.

_____

_____ 2. On every Saturday for the last two months, two sisters have gotten into an argument about what television show to watch. Both have ended up restricted to their rooms for the afternoon.

_____

_____ 3. Connor sits right behind Julie. He pops and smacks his gum all period. Julie is annoyed by him because she cannot pay attention.

_____

_____ 4. Twelve people were taken out of their morning classes and sent home because they have head lice.

_____

_____ 5. Paige set up a plan that one of her friends would only do the math homework. Another friend would only do science, and so on. Then, everybody would copy from each other.

_____

Activity 6
Use with Chapter 2, Lesson 3

Chapter 2

_____ **6.** At the meeting, Jesse is sitting in complete silence with his arms folded.

_____

_____ **7.** All of a sudden, Jill started wearing a new, fancy outfit every day.

_____

_____ **8.** Crystal's father got a new job, and she had to move to a different state.

_____

_____ **9.** Erica is overwhelmed with pressure to get good grades, do well on the volleyball team, and write for the school newspaper.

_____

_____ **10.** A friend of yours at school was recently in a car accident. The other driver, who ran into him, was driving while intoxicated.

_____

Applying Health Skills

Chapter 2

Stress Management

Your Body's Response to Change

Stress is your body's response to change. Some stress is positive and can give you energy. Other stress can be challenging.

Read each situation in the chart below. Write the cause(s) of the stress in the second column. Then write the stress management technique that could help each teen.

Situation	Cause(s) of Stress	Stress Management Technique
1. Christopher has put off starting his science project until the night before it is due. Now it is 10:00 and he is tired, in a panic, and does not even know where to begin.		
2. Megan has been hearing her parents fight at night after she goes to bed. She is worried that they are going to get a divorce. As a result, she has not been able to eat lately and is losing weight.		
3. During the winter, Justin broke his leg skiing. Unable to get physical activity for a period of time, he gained weight. Now that the cast is off, and he is able to move again, he is worried that his weight gain will keep him from making the baseball team.		
4. Amanda has changed schools in the middle of the year and is having a hard time making new friends. She had been an excellent student in her previous school, but she is having a hard time adjusting to her new surroundings and is now failing math.		

Chapter 3 Study Guide
Mental and Emotional Health

Study Tips
✔ Read the chapter objectives.
✔ Look up any unfamiliar words.
✔ Read the questions below before you read the chapter.

As you read the chapter, answer the following questions. Later you can use this guide to review the information in the chapter.

Lesson 1

1. Name four signs of good mental and emotional health.

_____

_____

_____

_____

2. What influences your self-concept?

_____

_____

3. How can you improve your mental and emotional health?

_____

_____

_____

Lesson 2

4. Describe the feeling of jealousy.

_____

5. What is the difference between anxiety and panic?

_____

_____

Chapter 3

Chapter 3 Study Guide
Mental and Emotional Health

6. How can you meet your three emotional needs?

_____

_____

_____

_____

_____

Lesson 3

7. What is a *stressor?*

_____

8. What does your body release during the fight-or-flight response?

_____

9. Name three relaxation techniques that can help manage stress.

_____

_____

_____

Lesson 4

10. Define *grief reaction.*

_____

_____

11. Describe the yearning stage of a grief reaction.

_____

_____

12. What are coping strategies?

_____

_____

Activity 7
Use with Chapter 3, Lesson 1

Your Mental and Emotional Health

People with good mental and emotional health have a positive outlook on life, accept themselves and others, and adapt to new situations. **Personality, self-concept, and self-esteem** are factors related to mental and emotional health.

Read the descriptions below. Then, write the factor being described in the space provided.

1. The unique combination of feelings, thoughts, and behaviors that make you

   different from everyone else is your _____.

2. _____ is described as positive or negative.

3. _____ can stand in the way of setting goals if it is negative.

4. _____ can be high or low.

5. How much you value yourself is your _____.

6. _____ can be increased by listing strengths.

7. Some people have a shy _____ while others do not.

8. The view you have of yourself is your _____.

9. Your _____ is healthy if you can accept that you make mistakes sometimes and can learn from them and move on.

10. You feel valued and appreciated when your _____ is high.

11. When you are disappointed, you can bounce back emotionally, or show resilience, if your _____ is high.

12. Your _____ can become more positive when you accomplish work.

13. The way you believe others see you affects your _____.

14. Your positive _____ gives you the confidence to work toward goals and achieve them.

15. Your _____ can be influenced in a positive or negative way in response to actions and remarks made by family, teachers, and other important people in your life.

Chapter 3

Activity 8
Use with Chapter 3, Lesson 2

Emotions

Emotions show how you feel. They can be expressed in healthy or unhealthy ways. Emotions can serve a positive or a negative function in your life.

Describe the positive side, the negative side, and a healthy way to express each of the emotions identified below.

The Good Side

Understanding Anger

_____
_____
_____
_____
_____
_____
_____

The Bad Side

The Good Side

Understanding Anxiety

_____
_____
_____
_____
_____
_____
_____

The Bad Side

The Good Side

Understanding Fear

_____
_____
_____
_____
_____
_____
_____

The Bad Side

Chapter 3

Activity 9
Use with Chapter 3, Lesson 3

Stress Management

Imagine that you represent a counseling service. You have been given the job of writing "infomercials," telling people how your counseling service can help them deal with the stressors of life. An infomercial is a commercial that provides information and expresses a specific viewpoint.

Write infomercials for any three stressors listed below.

List of Stressors

Taking a test

Playing in a championship game

Living with an annoying family member

Changing schools

Being chased almost every day by the vicious dog who lives next door

Getting into an argument with a long-time friend

Finding out a friend has been talking about you in a mean way

Your infomercial must include:

1. A description of the stressor
2. What can happen if people do not deal with this stressor in a healthy way
3. Solutions that your counseling service will help people use

Activity 10
Use with Chapter 3, Lesson 4

Stages of Grief

When someone you know suffers a loss, you can help by understanding the person's emotional needs. One way to do this is to recognize the person's stage in the grief process. Often, the best thing you can do is to just be there, listen, and understand, allowing the grieving person to express what he or she needs.

Read the following descriptions of people who have suffered a loss. Write the stage of grief they are in and an appropriate thing you could say.

1. Manuel's grandmother has just died. He keeps saying that he cannot believe his grandmother is really gone.

   Stage: _____

2. Jared was told that he did not make the football team. He is blaming his father, saying that his father did not teach him to pass the ball correctly.

   Stage: _____

3. Nicole's father has cancer. Nicole shares all of the details about his treatments and the changes in her family's life. Then, she lists all of the future events in her life that her father will miss, like her graduation and wedding.

   Stage: _____

4. Ali had a long, intense argument with her best friend Erica. Ali said things that she regrets—things Erica told her were unforgivable. Now Erica is not speaking to her, and Ali is deeply sad.

   Stage: _____

Chapter 3 Health Inventory

Rate Your Mental and Emotional Total Health

Read the statements below. In the space at the left, write *yes* if the statement describes you, or *no* if it does not describe you.

_____ 1. I am interested in other people.

_____ 2. I face my problems rather than avoid them.

_____ 3. I can laugh at myself.

_____ 4. I know my limits as well as my abilities.

_____ 5. I like who I am.

_____ 6. I see challenges as opportunities for growth.

_____ 7. I set realistic goals for myself.

_____ 8. I am satisfied with my effort if I have done my best.

_____ 9. I can cope with disappointment.

_____ 10. I can give and accept compliments.

_____ 11. I am comfortable about expressing my feelings.

_____ 12. I continue to participate in an activity even if I do not always get my way.

_____ 13. I can say no to people without feeling guilty.

_____ 14. I enjoy my own company.

_____ 15. I can ask for help when I need it.

Score yourself:

How many *yes* answers did you have? Write the number here.

12–15: You have excellent mental and emotional health.

8–11: Your mental and emotional health is good.

5–7: Your mental and emotional health is fair, but it could be better.

Fewer than 5: Reread Chapter 3 carefully to see what changes you can make to improve your mental and emotional health.

Chapter 3

Chapter 4 Study Guide
Mental and Emotional Problems

> ## Study Tips
> ✔ Read the chapter objectives.
> ✔ Look up any unfamiliar words.
> ✔ Read the questions below before you read the chapter.

As you read the chapter, answer the following questions. Later you can use this guide to review the information in the chapter.

Lesson 1

1. What are some characteristics of panic disorder?

_____

_____

_____

_____

2. What is a phobia? Name two examples of phobias.

_____

_____

_____

3. What are some characteristics of borderline personality disorder?

_____

_____

_____

_____

_____

4. How can schizophrenia be treated?

_____

Chapter 4 Study Guide
Mental and Emotional Problems

Lesson 2

5. What is *suicide?*

_____

6. How are depression and suicide related?

_____

7. What are some examples of self-destructive behaviors that could be warning signs of suicide?

_____

_____

8. What are some things to remember if you are ever thinking about suicide?

_____

_____

_____

Lesson 3

9. List some adults a teen might be able to trust and talk to about his or her mental or emotional problems?

_____

_____

10. What is *therapy?*

_____

11. What is *family therapy?*

_____

_____

12. What is a *clinical social worker?*

_____

_____

Chapter 4

Activity 11
Use with Chapter 4, Lesson 1

Mental and Emotional Disorders

Read the following descriptions of people who have mental and emotional disorders. On the line provided, write the diagnosis from the box that is being described.

Panic Disorder	Borderline Personality Disorder
Obsessive-Compulsive Disorder	Schizophrenia
Post-Traumatic Stress Disorder	Bipolar Disorder
Phobia	Depression
Passive-Aggressive Personality Disorder	

1. Ann cannot step on cracks on the floor or on the sidewalk. When people try to force her to put her foot on a crack, she becomes intensely fearful and screams. She is irritable and tense most of the time.

   _____

2. John goes to the emergency room frequently with shortness of breath and trembling. He believes he is having a heart attack.

   _____

3. Kayla has a difficult time cooperating with people. She complains about teachers, saying that they boss her around. She admits that she has not finished one assignment all term. At home she gets very angry when her parents punish her. Although she refuses to go any-where with her family, she accuses them of leaving her out of things.

   _____

4. Will hears voices. He is so distracted by these voices that he does not listen to what is actually said in class. Will does not say much to any-one, and admits that he does not trust people at all.

   _____

5. Sometimes Katherine talks constantly in a loud voice. She is unable to sit still and annoys everyone by walking around touching every-thing in sight. Other times, Katherine stays in bed all day. She insists that her life is hopeless.

   _____

Chapter 4

Activity 12

Use with Chapter 4, Lesson 2

Suicide

Place a check mark beside every statement that could be a warning sign of suicide.

1. Sue believes her life is worthless.	
2. Jan is not depressed.	
3. Tim has a positive outlook on his future.	
4. Ann feels a strong connection to her family and friends. She appreciates their support.	
5. Sam says things like, "No one cares if I live or die."	
6. Kelsey is extremely careful not to engage in any risky behaviors and will not do anything that might hurt her.	
7. Juan has withdrawn from all his friends and does not take part in any of the activities that he used to enjoy.	
8. Alexandra says that she could care less about what she looks like, or if she ever goes out with people she knows again.	
9. Andy talks about death, writes about death, and asks people odd questions about death.	
10. Natalie believes that if she tries her best, even if she sometimes fails, she will be happy.	
11. Cameron knows that he has made mistakes in school lately, but he says he has learned from the mistakes and will do better next term.	
12. Stephanie gave away all of her jewelry and cute clothes, telling people that they could remember her when they wore her things.	
13. After months of being deeply depressed and hardly talking to anyone, Evan suddenly became cheerful and seemed like he knew what he wanted.	

Chapter 4

Activity 13
Use with Chapter 4, Lesson 3

Mental Health Questions

Imagine that you are a licensed clinical social worker who answers questions once a week on a radio talk show. People call in with questions about mental and emotional disorders. The topic this week is: "Should I be worried if …?" You will listen to the symptoms the caller describes and determine if he or she has a serious problem.

Read what the caller says and write *Yes* on the line if the caller has a serious problem and *No* if the caller does not. Then, write a sentence that states the reason for your response.

What the caller said:	Should the caller be worried?	Your reason:
1. "During the last months, I've stopped eating regular meals because I'm never hungry. I stay awake most of the night, walking around the house. I'm failing some of my classes at school. I feel nervous all the time."		
2. "My therapist has recommended that I join his therapy group one night a week. He claims that the other people in the group will understand my problem and help me think of solutions."		
3. "I have felt suicidal for the last year and do not like leaving my house. I stopped going to counseling because my aunt has told me that as long as I took my medication, I did not need to discuss my problems."		
4. "I have not told anyone that I sleep most of the day. I have stopped speaking to my parents and my friends. There's no point in going to school since I'm failing anyway."		
5. "I was given medication by my doctor for a chemical imbalance. I stopped taking them because I don't want to be on drugs."		
6. "I argue with my mother every day. Our family doctor has set up family therapy for us. I know I will be expected to talk about my feelings."		

Chapter 4

Applying Health Skills

Decision Making

How to Help A Friend

Read the following paragraph. Then, imagine you are Matt's friend. Applying the decision-making skills to the situation, fill in the six steps in the decision-making strategy that you would use to help Matt.

When Matt heard last month that his family would be moving across the country at the end of the school year, he was excited. Now, however, he seems depressed and does not want to talk about the move. Nothing that used to interest him seems to make him happy anymore. When you suggest an activity, he says, "I don't care." You are worried about Matt's mental health. You feel he may be showing some of the warning signs of suicide, but you are afraid to talk to him about it.

Apply the decision-making skills to Matt's situation and demonstrate how you would help your friend.

1. State the situation.

_____

2. List the options.

_____

_____

3. Weigh the possible outcomes.

_____

_____

4. Consider your values.

_____

5. Make a decision and act.

_____

6. Evaluate the decision.

_____

Chapter 4

Chapter 5 Study Guide
Relationships: The Teen Years

> ### Study Tips
> ✔ Read the chapter objectives.
> ✔ Look up any unfamiliar words.
> ✔ Read the questions below before you read the chapter.

As you read the chapter, answer the following questions. Later you can use this guide to review the information in the chapter.

Lesson 1

1. What does sympathetic mean?

_____

_____

2. What is peer pressure?

_____

_____

3. What should a dating relationship be based on?

_____

_____

Lesson 2

4. What is communication?

_____

_____

5. What is an "I" message, and why is it effective?

_____

_____

_____

_____

Chapter 5 Study Guide
Relationships: The Teen Years

6. What is active listening?

_____

_____

Lesson 3

7. What is indirect peer pressure?

_____

_____

_____

8. In what ways can peer pressure be positive?

_____

_____

_____

9. What are refusal skills, and what can they help you do?

_____

_____

_____

Lesson 4

10. What are consequences?

_____

_____

11. What is abstinence?

_____

_____

12. Who can you talk to if you need help managing sexual feelings?

_____

_____

Chapter 5

Activity 14
Use with Chapter 5 Lesson 1

Send a Greeting

Teens sometimes use greeting cards to express their feelings. Imagine that you have become a creator of greeting cards.

Select any 2 of the topics listed below and create a greeting card for each. Draw the cover of the card and write the message that would go inside.

1. A good-bye card for a friend who is moving away.
2. An appreciation card for a good friend.
3. A sympathy card for a person who got in trouble because he was influenced by negative peer pressure.
4. A celebration card for your friend whose team won the championship.
5. An apology card to a dear friend.

Chapter 5

Activity 15
Use with Chapter 5, Lesson 2

Communication Skills

Read the descriptions of conversations in the first column. Then complete the chart with the communication skill being used.

Using body language as an aid	Expressing a clear message
Using intonation to send a message	Mirroring what was said
Active listening	Using an "I" message
Using a "conversation encourager"	

Conversation	Communication Skill
1. The speaker uses a firm tone of voice.	
2. The listener responds, "Wow, then what happened?"	
3. The speaker opens his arms and smiles.	
4. The speaker says, "I am angry because I heard that you were talking about me."	
5. The speaker maintains eye contact with the person to whom he is speaking.	
6. When the speaker paused, the listener said, "I understand that you believe Fred is in danger."	
7. The listener paid careful attention to what was said and nodded his head from time to time.	
8. The speaker said, "I am sure there has been a mistake and I do not owe you money."	

Chapter 5

Activity 16
Use with Chapter 5, Lesson 3

Benefit or Danger?

Complete the chart below by defining each term and identifying either the benefit or the danger of the term. The first term is done for you.

Term	Definition	Benefit	Danger
1. Positive Peer Pressure	A force that influences you to do what is right or to do your best, so you will be accepted by your peer group	It helps people by motivating them to do what is right or beneficial for them.	
2. Negative Peer Pressure			
3. Refusal Skills			
4. STOP Strategy			
5. Aggressive			
6. Passive			
7. Assertive			
8. "Lines"			

Chapter 5

Activity 17
Use with Chapter 5, Lesson 4

Healthful Behaviors

List as many benefits as you can find for each of the following concepts.

Concept	Benefits
1. Rules	
2. Limits, Invisible Boundaries	
3. Consequences	
4. Sexual Abstinence	
5. Affection without Sexual Intimacy	
6. Delaying Parenthood until Adulthood	

Chapter 5

Chapter 5 Health Inventory

Rate Your Relationships

Read the statements below. In the space at the left, write *yes* **if the statement describes you, or** *no* **if it does not describe you..**

_____ 1. I always try to be myself.

_____ 2. My friends and I respect each other's opinions.

_____ 3. My friends know that I care about them.

_____ 4. I express affection in healthy ways.

_____ 5. My friends and I trust each other.

_____ 6. I am sympathetic when bad things happen to my friends.

_____ 7. My friends and I can depend on one another.

_____ 8. I try to have a positive influence on my friends and peers.

_____ 9. I am able to make new friends.

_____ 10. I try to plan fun, safe activities with my friends.

_____ 11. I use refusal skills to avoid negative peer pressure.

_____ 12. I enjoy activities in a mixed group setting.

_____ 13. If I have dating relationships, they are based on caring and respect.

_____ 14. I understand the qualities of a good friend, and I always try to show them.

_____ 15. I know that no one is perfect, and I can forgive a friend's mistakes.

Score yourself:

How many *yes* answers did you circle? Write the number here.

11–15: You deserve top honors for your good friend and peer relationships.

6–10: You have average relationships with your friends and peers.

Fewer than 6: Changing some of your actions will allow you to have more valuable relationships with your friends and peers.

Chapter 5

Chapter 6 Study Guide
Promoting Social Health

Study Tips

✔ Read the chapter objectives.

✔ Look up any unfamiliar words.

✔ Read the questions below before you read the chapter.

As you read the chapter, answer the following questions. Later you can use this guide to review the information in the chapter.

Lesson 1

1. What is social health, and what is its foundation?

_____

_____

2. What is a role, and what are some of the different roles teens play?

_____

_____

3. In what ways can you show respect in your relationships?

_____

_____

4. In what ways can you show trust in your relationships?

_____

_____

Lesson 2

5. What is a single-parent family?

_____

6. What is an extended family?

_____

_____

Chapter 6

Chapter 6 Study Guide
Promoting Social Health

7. What are some of the ways families provide for social needs?

_____

_____

8. What are some ways families change due to circumstances?

_____

_____

_____

_____

_____

_____

Lesson 3

9. What is a commitment, and why is marriage such a large commitment?

_____

_____

_____

10. What is a divorce?

_____

11. What are some of the responsibilities of parenthood?

_____

_____

_____

_____

12. What are some health risks that can affect babies born from teen mothers?

_____

_____

Activity 18
Use with Chapter 6, Lesson 1

Healthy Relationships

Healthy relationships are built on the characteristics of:

1. Trust
2. Respect
3. Patience
4. Tolerance
5. Caring
6. Meeting the responsibilities of the role that you play in a relationship

Read the statements that describe healthy relationships. Beside each, write the characteristic(s) being described.

_____ 1. George accepts Marge's tendency to be late. He sits quietly and reads a magazine while he waits.

_____ 2. Sam knows that Jill will return the books that she is borrowing today, just as she has in the past.

_____ 3. When Jake goes to Kim's house, he leaves his shoes neatly in the hall by the front door, in the same way that all of the members of Kim's family leave their shoes.

_____ 4. When Matt does not eat sweets during the fasting period of his religion, Dan does not eat any sweets in front of Matt.

_____ 5. Courtney is careful not to interrupt Alyssa when she is speaking.

_____ 6. Jordan is a writer for the school newspaper. He makes it a point to hand in his articles on time so that they can be edited before the deadline.

_____ 7. Andy's photography teacher, who is Andy's best friend's older brother, just graduated from college and started teaching. Andy calls his teacher Mr. Sans, even though Mr. Sans is young, and Andy has known him for years.

_____ 8. Becky has never once repeated any of the private thoughts that her best friend Beth shares with her.

Chapter 6

Activity 19
Use with Chapter 6, Lesson 2

Families

Is this family getting along? At the end of each description, answer *Yes* or *No*. Then, give the reason for your view.

Description of a Family	Yes or No?	Your Reason
1. All of the family members help to take care of their elderly grandmother.		
2. Neither parent in this family cooks or shops for nutritious food, so the children just eat whatever snacks are around the house.		
3. Sasha and her mother are the only members of this family. They rarely have a conversation. Sasha feels as though her mother doesn't care about her.		
4. Jerry and his dad are the only members of this family. Every evening, over dinner, Jerry and his dad discuss their days at school and work.		
5. Whenever Gavin's dad is in a bad mood, he yells at Gavin.		
6. Cindy's mother and father work all day. Cindy refuses to babysit her younger sister after school, even though her parents expect her to.		
7. After Fran's mom died, Fran and her father met with the counselor at their church for support.		
8. After Trent's father lost his job, Trent had no money to go to the mall. His mother's paycheck was just enough to buy food and pay the bills.		
9. Two years after Ann's parents divorced, Ann's mother remarried. Her new husband moved in with his daughter. Now Ann is willing to share her room with her new stepsister.		
10. Matt's dad, a member of the National Guard, has been called into active duty and sent to the Middle East. Now, Matt has to do far more chores around the house.		

Chapter 6

Activity 20
Use with Chapter 6, Lesson 3

Successful Marriage and Family Life

Read version A and version B of the same situation. Then, decide which version shows the more successful marriage and family. On the lines below the versions, write the version you prefer and three reasons this version is better.

1. Monday morning with Amy and Rod

Version A	Version B
The alarm rings and both Amy and Rod get out of bed and go downstairs. Amy fixes coffee and a quick breakfast while Rod packs lunches for both of them. While they eat, they quietly discuss which bills they will pay. While Rod is dressing for work, Amy puts chicken and vegetables in a crock pot, so dinner will be ready when they get home, and they'll have time to watch a movie together. While Amy gets ready, Rod pays the bills that they agreed to pay. Then, he starts the car, so it will be warm for Amy. Together, looking forward to the evening, they leave for work.	The alarm rings and Amy gets up. She goes downstairs and fixes coffee and a quick breakfast while Rod continues to sleep. She calls to him, but he ignores her. She returns upstairs, calls a few more times, and finally starts getting ready for work. When she returns to the bedroom, he still is not up. She starts yelling, telling him how lazy he is. Rod finally gets up, and Amy goes downstairs. She is too upset to eat, so she decides to pay bills and discovers someone has spent extra money. When she goes back upstairs, yelling again, both lie and say the other spent the money on expensive lunches. Both leave for work without saying good-bye.

_____

_____

Chapter 6

2. Watching television with Barbara, Dan, and their three sons

Version A	**Version B**

Version A

Dan cooks dinner while Barbara watches television with the boys. The boys are fighting, and Barbara is yelling at them to stop. Finally, Dan joins them, but he is in a bad mood because the boys will not eat. Dan decides to watch the news, but cannot hear it because the youngest boy is whining and the other two are teasing him. The oldest boy remembers that he has homework, but says that he is too tired. Dan is too tired to argue, so he finds a program they all like. Barbara cannot watch though because the kitchen is a mess and no laundry is sorted. While Dan carries the sleeping younger boys up to bed, Barbara is left downstairs complaining and miserable. To avoid a fight, Dan ignores her and goes to bed.

Version B

The boys are seated at the kitchen table doing their homework while Barbara and Dan fix dinner. Dan helps his oldest son with his assignment, and the other boys take turns giving each other spelling checks. Finally, all homework is done and Barbara serves dinner. The house rule is that the television does not go on until all homework is completed, everyone has eaten, and all chores are done. Dan wants to watch the news, so he cleans the kitchen while Barbara and the boys sort laundry. The boys bring their own clothes up to their rooms, so they can watch their favorite program that comes on after the news. Before going to bed, each member of the family shares one thing about his or her day.

Chapter 6

Applying Health Skills

Communication Skills

Family Communication

Directions: With other students, take turns using and evaluating good communication skills in family conversations.

1. Form a group with two other students. Each of you will participate in two different conversations and observe one conversation.

2. When it is your turn to participate in a conversation, choose one of these topics. Circle the topic you and your partner have chosen. (You will do this twice, once with each of the other students in your group.)
   - A day my brother needed my help
   - Something I did for my sister
   - A funny family story
   - What I have learned from my parents
   - What is most important to my family
   - A problem our family solved

3. With your partner, hold a one-minute conversation on the topic you have chosen. Use good communication skills in your conversation.

4. When it is your turn to observe a conversation, use this checklist. Check off each communication skill you observe the other two group members using in their conversation.

Speaking Skills		Listening Skills	
"I" messages		Appropriate body language	
Clear, simple statements		Conversation encouragers	
Honest thoughts and feelings		Mirror thoughts and feelings	
Appropriate body language		Ask questions	

5. After each conversation, discuss which communication skills were used.

6. Which communication skills did you use most often in your two conversations?

   _____

7. Which communication skills do you need to practice?

   _____

Chapter 6

Chapter 7 Study Guide
Conflict Resolution

Study Tips

✔ Read the chapter objectives.

✔ Look up any unfamiliar words.

✔ Read the questions below before you read the chapter.

As you read the chapter, answer the following questions. Later you can use this guide to review the information in the chapter.

Lesson 1

1. What are some different issues that can cause conflicts?

_____

_____

_____

2. What are some common places where conflicts occur, and who are these conflicts usually with?

_____

_____

_____

_____

3. What is a bully?

_____

_____

4. What are conflicts with brothers and sisters usually about?

_____

_____

_____

_____

_____

Chapter 7 Study Guide
Conflict Resolution

Lesson 2

5. Name some factors or emotions that fuel conflict.

6. What are some healthy ways to deal with anger?

7. What are some of the negative consequences of jealousy, and what are some healthy ways to deal with jealousy?

8. Why is putting yourself in someone else's situation a good way to keep conflicts from escalating?

Lesson 3

9. What is mediation, and when should it be used?

Chapter 7

Chapter 7 Study Guide
Conflict Resolution

10. What are some qualities to look for in a mediator?

_____

_____

_____

_____

11. Why is the win-win solution the best kind of solution to a conflict?

_____

_____

12. Why do teens make good mediators for their peers?

_____

_____

_____

_____

Activity 21
Use with Chapter 7, Lesson 1

Understanding the Causes of Conflict

Knowing the cause of a conflict often helps people find an effective way to deal with the conflict.

Read the description of conflicts in the first column. In the next column, write the reason for the conflict. In the last column, write a healthy way to deal with the conflict.

Conflict	Reason	Healthy Way to Deal With the Conflict
1. Your mom insists that you come directly home after school and complete all homework before you see your friends. You can not go out after dinner on school nights. You are angry with your mother, but do not say anything.		
2. Your sister's boyfriend uses your video games without asking.		
3. Your teacher will not allow you to talk to your friends or write notes while he is teaching. You have had several detentions and missed track practice. Now your track coach is annoyed with you.		
4. A group of girls makes unkind remarks about your clothes and shoes every day when you walk down the hall.		
5. Several students in your chemistry class have accused you of stealing chemicals. They talk about people of your race being thieves and drug dealers.		
6. Every day when you sit down at the lunch table, a group of girls walks by and takes food off your tray, saying things like "You don't need any more calories!"		

Activity 22
Use with Chapter 7, Lesson 2

The Truth About Preventing Conflicts

Some of the following statements about preventing conflicts are facts and others are not. Classify each statement by writing *true* or *false* in the space at the left. Correct the ones you have identified as false on the lines that follow the statements.

_____ **1.** A first step in preventing conflicts from turning violent is recognizing that a conflict is building.

_____

_____

_____ **2.** Seeking revenge always helps a jealous person get what he or she wants.

_____

_____

_____ **3.** When a fight is developing, encouraging those involved shows good character.

_____

_____

_____ **4.** Two emotions that fuel conflict are anger and jealousy.

_____

_____

_____ **5.** Drinking alcohol helps most people deal with conflict in a healthier way.

_____

_____

_____ **6.** Learning to accept and appreciate people who are different from you can help prevent conflict.

_____

_____

_____ **7.** Mob mentality is an example of group pressure.

_____

_____

Activity 23
Use with Chapter 7, Lesson 3

Conflict Resolution and Mediation

Complete the charts below by filling in the missing steps in the conflict resolution and mediation processes. Then, list the characteristics of good mediators and a win-win outcome in the boxes provided.

The Conflict Resolution Process

Step 1	Take a time-out, calming down 30 minutes before discussion.
Step 2	A
Step 3	L
Step 4	K

The Mediation Process

First	Find a private location. The only people present should be a _____ and _____.
Second	
Sometimes	The mediator has to _____ _____.
Finally	

Characteristics of Good Mediators

1.	
2.	
3.	
4.	
5.	

Characteristics of a Win-Win Situation

6.	
7.	

Chapter 7 Health Inventory

Conflict Prevention and Resolution

Read the statements below. In the space at the left, write *yes* if the statement describes you, or *no* if it does not describe you.

_____ 1. I know that seeking help can prevent conflict.

_____ 2. I respect the values of other people.

_____ 3. When I feel my emotions running high, I step away from the situation.

_____ 4. When I am angry, I take a moment to be quiet and feel my anger.

_____ 5. I am able to share my feelings calmly and responsibly.

_____ 6. I know that alcohol and other drugs can contribute to conflict.

_____ 7. When I feel jealous of someone, I speak to a trusted adult about my feelings or write in my journal.

_____ 8. I can accept and appreciate people who are different from me.

_____ 9. I show respect for myself and others.

_____ 10. I try putting myself in other people's situations.

_____ 11. If I have a conflict with someone, I try to keep it private and not involve others.

_____ 12. If someone has hurt me, I do not seek revenge.

_____ 13. I try my best to get along peacefully with everyone.

_____ 14. If someone tries to bully me, I walk away and share the matter with a trusted adult.

_____ 15. I do not label people.

Score yourself:

Write the number of *yes* answers here.

12–15: You are well informed about preventing and resolving conflicts.

8–11: You are beginning to get the message.

Fewer than 8: You still need to learn more about preventing and resolving conflicts.

Chapter 8 Study Guide
Violence Prevention

Study Tips
✔ Read the chapter objectives.
✔ Look up any unfamiliar words.
✔ Read the questions below before you read the chapter.

As you read the chapter, answer the following questions. Later you can use this guide to review the information in the chapter.

Lesson 1

1. Define *drug trafficking.*

_____

2. Identify three factors that influence teen violence.

_____

_____

Lesson 2

3. What are two violent crimes that often occur together?

_____

4. How can a person avoid becoming a rape victim?

_____

5. What are two ways you can help to prevent violence?

_____

_____

Lesson 3

6. What is intimidation?

_____

_____

Chapter 8 Study Guide
Violence Prevention

7. List four ways to deal with harassment.

_____

_____

_____

_____

Lesson 4

8. Define domestic violence.

_____

9. In the case of sexual abuse, who is usually the abuser?

_____

_____

10. What are some of the self-destructive behaviors that victims of abuse sometimes experience?

_____

_____

_____

Lesson 5

11. How can victims break the cycle of abuse?

_____

_____

12. Where can victims of abuse go to if they feel they are in danger?

_____

_____

Activity 24
Use with Chapter 8, Lesson 1

Causes of Violence

In the chart below, list how each of the factors on the left can contribute to violence.

Factor	How The Factor Causes Violence
1. Media	
2. Gangs	
3. Availability of Weapons	
4. Drugs	

5. Make a sign with a slogan to carry at a stop-the-violence rally.

Activity 25
Use with Chapter 8, Lesson 2

Dealing With Violence

Imagine that you are a police officer who will speak at an assembly on dealing with violence. You have prepared your notes on assault and battery, rape, being attacked, and stopping violence.

Complete the note cards below.

The Way Assault and Battery Go Together:

1. _____
   _____
   _____
   _____
   _____

The Most Common Victims are:

2.

3.

The Facts about Rape:

7.

8.

9.

If attacked, the 3 Things a Person Should Do:

4.

5.

6.

The Ways to Avoid Rape:

10.

11.

12.

13.

What You Can Do to Stop Violence:

14.

15.

Activity 26
Use with Chapter 8, Lesson 3

Harassment Hot Line

Imagine that you work for a harassment hot line. Your job is to answer questions, offer explanations, and make suggestions to the people who call.

Write an answer on the lines provided to each of the following call-in questions.

Caller # 1: In math class I sit at a table of boys. When we have group assignments, these boys will not allow me to participate. They say girls cannot solve problems. What should I do?

_____

_____

Caller # 2: Every day the same group of girls messes up my hair and touch my arms. I am a guy who likes girls, but I do not like this. Please explain.

_____

_____

Caller # 3: Yesterday, a group of rough kids walked very close to me— too close. Then, they said things like, "We'll get you later," and "Sure hope you can fight." I'm not big or strong. What should I do?

_____

_____

Caller # 4: I'm a girl. This morning in a doorway, a boy blocked my way by standing so close to me that I would have to brush against him to get out the door. Luckily, the bell rang and he ran off. What was his problem?

_____

_____

Caller # 5: Some girls I know enjoy making fun of my pale skin. They ask questions like, "Were you born in a cave?" or "Do you live under a rock?" How should I respond?

_____

_____

Activity 27

Use with Chapter 8, Lesson 4

Truths and Myths About Abuse

Read each of the following statements about abuse. If the statement is accurate, check it. If it is not accurate, correct it in the space provided.

Statements	Check	Corrections
1. Victims of abuse often blame themselves.		
2. Enabling causes domestic abuse because the victim threatens the abuser with criminal charges, creating tension.		
3. Emotional abuse involves physical harm to a victim, so the victim feels helpless.		
4. During school, sexual abuse that includes jokes, gestures, and notes of a sexual nature should be ignored.		
5. Sometimes abusers use bribes to persuade a child to perform sexual acts.		
6. In domestic abuse cases, the abuser may seek to maintain authority over the family by pushing and slapping.		
7. There is no help for victims of abuse. The damage has been done and the scars remain.		
8. Fortunately, emotional abuse is forgotten quickly.		
9. There are few cases of American children being neglected. Americans tend to spoil their children.		
10. Abuse of teenagers is mainly a problem of people living in poverty.		
11. Enabling establishes a pattern of abuse.		
12. People who have been abused may develop self-destructive behaviors.		

Activity 28
Use with Chapter 8, Lesson 5

Help For Abuse

Complete each sentences using the words in the box.

crisis hot line	emotional trauma
cycle	help
enablers	fear
shelters	abuse
sexual	group counseling sessions

1. Whenever _____ is present in a family, all members are affected.

2. Some abused people are considered _____ because they conceal the abuse.

3. The _____ of abuse is a pattern of abuse that goes back generations because children who experience abuse see this behavior as a model of how to live.

4. A _____ is a toll-free telephone service where abuse victims can get help.

5. If abuse is _____, people may feel ashamed and find reporting the abuse uncomfortable.

6. Victims of abuse may _____ that telling about the abuse will lead to the break-up of their family.

7. In spite of promises to stop, the only way an abuser will ever stop is to get _____.

8. Victims of abuse need help getting over the _____ of their abuse.

9. Sometimes abuse victims need to go to _____ for protection.

10. _____ provide a chance for victims of abuse to discuss their situation with others who have experienced similar problems.

Applying Health Skills

Chapter 8

Practicing Healthful Behaviors

Protecting Yourself

With other students, create and perform a skit about ways to prevent violence.

1. With your partner or group, list at least five ways to prevent violence.

_____

_____

_____

_____

_____

2. Plan a short skit in which the characters discuss or demonstrate ways to prevent violence. Use the ideas you have listed above. Write a brief description of the situation, the characters, and the action of your skit.

_____

_____

_____

_____

_____

3. Together, practice acting out your skit.

4. Perform your skit for the rest of the class.

Chapter 9 Study Guide
Physical Activity and Fitness

Study Tips
✔ Read the chapter objectives.
✔ Look up any unfamiliar words.
✔ Read the questions below before you read the chapter.

As you read the chapter, answer the following questions. Later you can use this guide to review the information in the chapter.

Lesson 1

1. Why is physical activity important?

_____

_____

2. Name three characteristics of people who are physically fit.

_____

_____

_____

3. Define *anaerobic exercise* and name two examples.

_____

_____

_____

Lesson 2

4. Name three exercises that can improve your muscle strength and muscle endurance.

_____

_____

5. What instrument is used to measure body composition?

_____

6. How can a positive attitude improve your physical fitness?

_____

_____

Lesson 3

7. What is cross-training and why is it beneficial?

_____

_____

_____

8. Why is creating a fitness schedule so important?

_____

_____

_____

9. What does FITT stand for?

_____

Lesson 4

10. Define *conditioning* and name three ways athletes can condition themselves.

_____

_____

_____

_____

11. Why is it so important to drink plenty of water when exercising or playing a sport?

_____

_____

_____

Chapter 9 Study Guide
Physical Activity and Fitness

12. Name three ways to minimize your risk of injury when exercising or playing a sport.

_____

_____

_____

_____

_____

Chapter 9

Activity 29
Use with Chapter 9, Lesson 1

The Effects of Exercise

Write the specific effects of regular physical activity in each of the boxes below.

Effects

Regular Physical Activity	1. On Physical Health

Regular Physical Activity	2. On Social Health

Regular Physical Activity	3. On Mental and Emotional Health

Physical Fitness	4. Provides:

Aerobic Exercise	5. Benefits:

Anaerobic Exercise	6. Builds:

Activity 30
Use with Chapter 9, Lesson 2

Endurance, Strength, and Flexibility

Complete the following sentences, writing your responses on the blanks provided.

1. Doctors measure blood pressure to _____
_____ .

2. Doctors measure heart and lung endurance to see _____
_____ .

3. Muscle strength is _____
_____ .

4. Muscle endurance is _____
_____ .

5. Weight lifting can be used to _____
_____ .

6. Swimming builds both heart and lung endurance and provides a _____
_____ .

7. You can endure if you can _____
_____ .

8. Flexibility is _____
_____ .

9. Body composition is _____
_____ .

10. You can improve your body composition by _____
_____ .

Activity 31
Use with Chapter 9, Lesson 3

Your Fitness Plan

Create your own fitness plan by filling in the chart below.

Steps	Your Plan
Step 1: Your goals:	
Step 2: Select the activities that you will do, including: Aerobic Exercises Anaerobic Exercises Cross-Training Activity Equipment that you will need	
Step 3: Determine your schedule: School Physical Activities Outside Activities that involve physical activity Plan to build up your activity gradually in terms of **F**requency **I**ntensity **T**ime **T**ype	
Step 4: Monitor your heart rate: Resting heart rate: Target heart rate:	
Step 5: The warm ups and cool downs that you intend to use:	

Activity 32

Sports Conditioning

Read the following descriptions related to sports conditioning. Identify the term that is being described and write the term on the line provided.

Knowing Limits	Treating Injuries
Weather-Related Injuries	Proper Gear
Sports Nutrition	Minimizing Risk

_____ 1. Eat carbohydrates like fruits, vegetables, and whole-grain products before a game or event. Avoid candy and other foods high in simple sugars.

_____ 2. Drink plenty of water, at least 8 ounces just before a game.

_____ 3. Progress in your activity gradually. Use warm ups and cooldowns.

_____ 4. Get the proper shoes and safety equipment.

_____ 5. Stop participating in the activity if you are in pain.

_____ 6. Use the PRICE formula to find relief from injury or muscle soreness.

_____ 7. Prevent dehydration and exhaustion.

_____ 8. Prevent frostbite and hypothermia.

Chapter 9

Chapter 9 Health Inventory

Physical Activity and Fitness

Read the statements below. In the space at the left, write *yes* if the statement describes you, or *no* if it does not describe you.

_____ **1.** I get 60 minutes of activity on most days.

_____ **2.** I am able to handle the stress and challenges of everyday life.

_____ **3.** I am comfortable in social situations.

_____ **4.** I have good endurance.

_____ **5.** I set goals to achieve a greater fitness level.

_____ **6.** I improve my flexibility by stretching, turning, and bending.

_____ **7.** I eat a well-balanced diet.

_____ **8.** I choose physical activities that I enjoy.

_____ **9.** I take advantage of the benefits of cross-training when I exercise.

_____ **10.** I always use protective gear if the activity requires it.

_____ **11.** I am practical and realistic in scheduling physical activity.

_____ **12.** I put my fitness plan in writing.

_____ **13.** I try my best to get along peacefully with everyone.

_____ **14.** I use the **FITT** principle to avoid injury.

_____ **15.** I always warm up and cool down.

Score yourself:

Write the number of *yes* answers here. [ ]

12–15: You are well informed about physical activity and fitness, and their benefits.

8–11: You are beginning to understand about physical activity and fitness, and their benefits.

Fewer than 8: You still need to learn more about physical activity and fitness, and their benefits.

Chapter 9

Chapter 10 Study Guide
Nutrition for Health

Study Tips

✔ Read the chapter objectives.

✔ Look up any unfamiliar words.

✔ Read the questions below before you read the chapter.

As you read the chapter, answer the following questions. Later you can use this guide to review the information in the chapter.

Lesson 1

1. What is nutrition?

_____

2. What is the difference between appetite and hunger?

_____

_____

3. Why do many people not get enough nutrients?

_____

_____

Lesson 2

4. What are the health benefits of eating fiber?

_____

_____

5. What are proteins made up of?

_____

6. Name three minerals that your body needs to function properly.

_____

_____

Chapter 10 Study Guide
Nutrition for Health

Lesson 3

7. What are the six sections in the MyPyramid food guidance system?

_____

_____

8. Why is it important to balance the calories you consume with physical activity?

_____

_____

9. What condition can an excess of sodium lead to?

_____

Lesson 4

10. Why is breakfast such an important meal?

_____

_____

11. How can you balance your eating plan? How can it help you?

_____

_____

_____

12. What should you look for when choosing a snack?

_____

_____

Activity 33

Food Choices

Many factors influence what foods we eat. Among these influences are *family and friends, cultural background, food availability, time and money resources, advertising, knowledge of nutrition,* and *personal preferences.* Read the following situations. Identify which factor or factors might have influenced the person's food choices.

Situation 1
Bethany is on a tight budget. She purchases many of the foods she eats based on whether or not she has a coupon for it. When she can, she splurges on foods she has seen in her favorite magazine.

_____

Situation 2
Sam's mother is a pediatrician. She tries to make sure that her family always eats nutritious meals.

_____

Situation 3
Myrna does not have much time for breakfast. She would have rather had a bagel, but the donut shop was out of bagels. She bought a sugar donut instead.

_____

Situation 4
Damien is a college student who does not have much money or time to cook. He has been eating a lot of pasta, beans, and vegetables.

_____

Situation 5
Yoshi's family is from Japan. Her family eats many dishes with fish and vegetables. Her mother also makes sushi often.

_____

Situation 6
On his way home from school every day, Dan stops at a convenience store. Instead of buying chips and soda, he always chooses a bottle of juice and a box of raisins.

_____

Chapter 10

Activity 34
Use with Chapter 10, Lesson 2

Letter Scramble

Unscramble the capitalized words in the sentences below. Then write the words on the lines at the left. On the numbered lines at the bottom of the page, write the boxed letters from the words you have unscrambled. They will form a two-word message.

1. ___ ___ ___ [ ] ___

2. ___ ___ [ ] ___ ___ ___ ___

3. ___ ___ [ ] ___ ___ ___ ___

4. ___ [ ] ___ ___ ___ ___ ___ ___ ___ ___

5. ___ ___ [ ] ___ ___ ___ ___

6. ___ [ ] ___ ___

7. ___ ___ [ ] ___ ___ ___

8. ___ ___ [ ] ___ ___ ___ ___

9. ___ ___ [ ] ___ ___

10. ___ ___ ___ ___ ___ [ ] ___ ___ ___ ___ ___ ___

1. REFIB is a special type of complex carbohydrate found in raw fruits, vegetables, and whole grains.

2. TIVMANIS help your body to fight infections.

3. SNIEPTOR are nutrients your body uses to build, repair, and maintain cells and tissues.

4. STRELOELOCH is a fatty substance found in the blood.

5. SLRANEMI are elements that help form healthy bones and teeth, and regulate certain body processes.

6. Saturated STAF are solid at room temperature.

7. BLEYRA is an example of a whole grain.

8. Foods like butter, cheese, and fatty meats are high in DETRAUTAS fats.

9. Amino acids are found in beef, pork, poultry, eggs, and IFHS.

10. BRACHODYATERS are sugars and starches that occur naturally in foods, mainly in plants.

____ ____ ____   ____ ____ ____ ____ ____ ____ ____ !

1   2   3   4   5   6   7   8   9   10

Chapter 10

Activity 35
Use with Chapter 10, Lesson 3

Knowing the Facts

Read each situation below, in which the teen described could make a healthier choice. In the space provided, write a better choice for the teen.

1. Lauren does not like vegetables. Most days her diet does not contain any foods from this food group.

   _____

   _____

2. Adam ate breakfast and lunch at his favorite fast food restaurant. Later, he was surprised to learn that his calorie intake for those two meals was 2,500 calories.

   _____

   _____

3. Christa was cutting vegetables for her family's dinner when she heard her dog barking from the backyard. She let the dog in, petted him, and went right back to preparing dinner.

   _____

   _____

4. Luis made himself a frozen pizza for lunch but only ate one quarter of it. He left the rest of the pizza out on the counter for his dad to eat when he got home for dinner.

   _____

   _____

5. The only kind of chicken Danielle will eat is chicken that has been deep fried.

   _____

   _____

Activity 36

Menu Planning

The key to a balanced eating plan is advanced planning. Prepare a menu plan for the next three days by completing the chart below. Use the MyPyramid illustration in your textbook for guidance.

Menu Plan

	Day 1	Day 2	Day 3
Breakfast			
Lunch			
Snack			
Dinner			

Chapter 10

Applying Health Skills

Advocacy

Eating for Your Health

With a group, plan and create a cartoon that encourages teens to make healthy food choices.

1. Think about how you can use a cartoon to convince teens that they should eat a variety of foods each day. List at least three facts about nutrition from Chapter 10 to support that idea.

_____

_____

_____

_____

_____

2. With the other members of your group, discuss how you can use a cartoon to present your idea and your supporting facts. Decide whether you will create a single-panel cartoon or a comic strip. Circle your group's choice.

        Single-Panel Cartoon   Comic Strip

3. Together, write a brief description of the cartoon you are planning.

_____

_____

_____

4. Work together to draw and write the cartoon you have planned. Use construction paper and markers or crayons.

5. Share your group's cartoon with the rest of the class.

Chapter 10

Chapter 11 Study Guide
Your Body Image

Study Tips
✔ Read the chapter objectives.
✔ Look up any unfamiliar words.
✔ Read the questions below before you read the chapter.

As you read the chapter, answer the following questions. Later you can use this guide to review the information in the chapter.

Lesson 1

1. How can you boost your body image?

_____

_____

_____

_____

2. Define *appropriate weight*.

_____

3. What factors determine your BMI?

_____

4. Why is the number of overweight American children and teens at an all-time high?

_____

_____

_____

5. What health risks are caused by being overweight?

_____

_____

6. How many calories should a moderately active male teen eat each day?

_____

Chapter 11

Chapter 11 Study Guide
Your Body Image

Lesson 2

7. What are eating disorders?

_____

_____

8. What is the most common eating disorder?

_____

9. What health concerns are associated with anorexia nervosa?

_____

_____

10. What age group is anorexia nervosa most common in?

_____

_____

11. How do people with bulimia nervosa purge the food they have eaten?

_____

_____

12. What are two signs that someone might have bulimia nervosa?

_____

_____

Chapter 11

Activity 37

Use with Chapter 11, Lesson 1

Two Eating Plans

Two eating plans are described below. Read the descriptions and answer the questions that follow.

Sara's Eating Plan

Sara wants to make sure she is ready for her gymnastics season. She has decided to have a boiled egg, grapefruit juice, and whole wheat toast for breakfast. For lunch, she will eat a piece of baked chicken leftover from last night's dinner with carrot and celery sticks. Her after-school snack will be a glass of low-fat milk and an apple. At dinner, she will eat healthful portions of whatever is prepared, but she will not have butter or sour cream on her potato, and she will have fruit for dessert instead of cake or cookies.

1. Is Sara's plan likely to be successful? Why or why not?

_____

_____

2. Explain what is healthful (or not) about Sara's plan, and what, if any, changes she should make.

_____

_____

Jared's Eating Plan

In order to make a weight class, Jared needs to lose 10 pounds before wrestling season starts. He has read about an all-protein diet guaranteed to take off 14 pounds in 14 days. Jared eats cottage cheese for breakfast, a cheeseburger for lunch, and a steak for dinner. As the diet instructs, he drinks eight glasses of water each day. He is dropping pounds but feels tired and grumpy all the time.

3. Is Jared's plan likely to be successful? Why or why not?

_____

_____

4. Explain what is healthful (or not) about Jared's plan and what changes, if any, he should make.

_____

5. Which eating plan is healthier?

_____

Chapter 11

Activity 38
Use with Chapter 11, Lesson 2

Eating Disorder Fact and Fiction

Some of the statements below are facts and others are not. Classify each by writing *fact* or *fiction* in the space at the left. On the lines that follow the statements, correct the ones you have identified as fiction.

_____ **1.** Females are the only victims of eating disorders.

_____

_____ **2.** Eating disorders are brought on by hunger.

_____

_____ **3.** Having an eating disorder places a person at risk for developing severe medical problems.

_____

_____ **4.** The most common eating disorder is anorexia nervosa.

_____

_____ **5.** Compulsive eaters eat even when they are not hungry.

_____

_____ **6.** People with anorexia need immediate help and unless they get it, they may die.

_____

_____ **7.** People with anorexia may think they are overweight, even if they are not.

_____

_____ **8.** People with bulimia purge food they have eaten by vomiting or taking laxatives.

_____

_____ **9.** Telling a trusted adult about a friend with an eating disorder is an act of betrayal.

_____

_____ **10.** People with bulimia usually become extremely thin.

_____

Chapter 11

Chapter 11 Health Inventory

Body Maintenance

Read each statement below. In the space at the left, write *yes* if the statement describes you, or *no* if it does not describe you.

_____ **1.** I focus on how I feel rather than how I look.

_____ **2.** I drink water or fruit juice instead of a soft drink when I'm thirsty.

_____ **3.** I talk to my doctor if I'm concerned about my weight.

_____ **4.** I avoid fad diets.

_____ **5.** I seek the support of family and friends when I'm feeling bad about my body or my weight.

_____ **6.** I set realistic goals for maintaining my weight.

_____ **7.** I feel good about my body.

_____ **8.** I am at an appropriate weight for my age, gender, height, and body frame.

_____ **9.** I avoid using food as a way to cope with depression or stress.

_____ **10.** I avoid eating fast food.

_____ **11.** I try to get regular physical activity every day.

_____ **12.** I try to limit my fat intake each day.

_____ **13.** I pay close attention to the nutrient value of the foods I eat.

_____ **14.** I base my food choices on the MyPyramid food guidelines.

_____ **15.** I pay attention to portion sizes when I am eating.

Score yourself:

Write the number of *yes* answers here. ☐

12–15: Excellent. You know how to manage your weight.

8–11: Good. You understand some of the issues necessary to manage your weight.

Fewer than 8: It would be a good idea to review Chapter 11 and learn more about managing your weight.

Chapter 11

Chapter 12 Study Guide
Alcohol

Study Tips

✔ Read the chapter objectives.

✔ Look up any unfamiliar words.

✔ Read the questions below before you read the chapter.

As you read the chapter, answer the following questions. Later you can use this guide to review the information in the chapter.

Lesson 1

1. List the problems that alcohol can cause for teens.

_____

_____

_____

2. What are some of the reasons why teens drink alcohol?

_____

_____

_____

_____

_____

3. What are some good alternatives to drinking alcohol?

_____

_____

_____

Lesson 2

4. What is reaction time? How does alcohol use affect a person's reaction time?

_____

_____

Chapter 12   Chapter 12 Alcohol   Teen Health   Course 3   **79**

Chapter 12 Study Guide
Alcohol

5. What happens when a person consumes more alcohol than his or her liver can process?

_____

_____

_____

6. What is alcohol poisoning?

_____

_____

_____

Lesson 3

7. In what ways can heavy alcohol use damage the stomach?

_____

_____

_____

_____

_____

8. What is binge drinking?

_____

_____

Lesson 4

9. What are the five major symptoms of alcoholism?

_____

_____

_____

Chapter 12

Chapter 12 Study Guide
Alcohol

10. What are the symptoms of alcohol abuse?

_____

_____

_____

_____

_____

Lesson 5

11. What is recovery?

_____

_____

12. What is the first step in an alcoholic's recovery process?

_____

_____

_____

Chapter 12

Activity 39

Say No, No, No to Alcohol

Resisting peer pressure can be very difficult at times. Listed below are several ways to say no to alcohol. Complete the remaining sentences by suggesting other ways to refuse alcohol.

1. No thanks, I'm allergic to alcohol.

2. No thanks, I'm in training for swim team.

3. No thanks, I can't use the car if I drink.

4. No thanks, I'm a member of SADD.

5. No thanks, _____

6. No thanks, _____

7. No thanks, _____

8. No thanks, _____

9. No thanks, _____

10. No thanks, _____

11. No thanks, _____

12. No thanks, _____

13. No thanks, _____

14. No thanks, _____

15. No thanks, _____

16. No thanks, _____

17. No thanks! _____

Chapter 12

Activity 40
Use with Chapter 12, Lesson 2

Alcohol Myths

Some of the statements below are facts and others are not. Classify each by writing *fact* or *myth* in the space at the left. On the lines that follow the statements, correct the ones you have identified as fiction.

_____ 1. Drinking alcohol is not as dangerous as taking drugs.

_____

_____ 2. Drinking alcohol makes you more attractive.

_____

_____ 3. The worst that drinking can do is leave you with a hangover.

_____

_____ 4. The same amount of alcohol has a greater effect on a small person than it does on a larger one.

_____

_____ 5. Alcohol generally moves into the bloodstream faster in females than males.

_____

_____ 6. Mixing alcohol with other drugs or medicines can cause death.

_____

_____ 7. Hard liquor gets you drunk faster than beer or wine.

_____

_____ 8. Two to three drinks can cause a loss of coordination and judgment.

_____

_____ 9. A cold shower and cup of coffee will take away the effects of alcohol.

_____

_____ 10. One of the greatest dangers of alcohol is its unpredictability.

_____

Chapter 12

Activity 41
Use with Chapter 12, Lesson 3

Alcohol's Effects

Match the descriptions in the left column with the part of the body adversely affected by alcohol use.

_____ 1. Alcohol is a depressant affecting a person's emotional health.

_____ 2. Alcohol is not digested like other foods. It is absorbed by tissues and goes directly into the blood. It is associated with cancer here.

_____ 3. A life-threatening problem associated with heavy alcohol use is cirrhosis.

_____ 4. Alcohol increases the amount of acid, making the lining of this part of the body red and swollen.

_____ 5. Alcohol can cause this to become enlarged.

_____ 6. Alcohol can cause this to shrink.

_____ 7. Alcohol interferes with this doing its job, which is to remove poisons from the blood.

_____ 8. Alcohol can affect memory and problem solving abilities.

a. mouth

b. stomach

c. liver

d. brain

e. heart

Answer the following questions about alcohol use. Write your answers on the lines provided.

9. Define *binge drinking* and list some of the dangers associated with it.

_____

_____

_____

10. Define *inhibition* and explain alcohol's likely effect on it.

_____

_____

_____

Chapter 12

Activity 42
Use with Chapter 12, Lesson 4

Treating Alcoholism

People who become alcoholics develop their drinking problems over a period of time. Experts have identified four distinct stages of alcoholism.

Read the statements below. Identify the stage of alcoholism each statement describes by writing 1, 2, 3, or 4 in the space to the left.

_____ **1.** Long periods of being intoxicated all the time.

_____ **2.** The drinker's body is strongly addicted to alcohol.

_____ **3.** A person starts using alcohol to relax or relieve stress.

_____ **4.** The drinker is often absent from school or work.

_____ **5.** The drinker begins to lie or make excuses about his or her drinking.

_____ **6.** Saying or doing hurtful things.

Answer the following questions about alcoholism. Write your answers on the lines provided.

7. What effects can alcoholism have on a family?

_____

8. How many families in the United States are affected by alcoholism?

_____

9. What are two support groups for families coping with alcoholism?

_____

_____

10. List the four steps of the recovery process and describe what each involves.

_____

_____

_____

_____

Chapter 12

Activity 43
Use with Chapter 12, Lesson 5

Help for the Alcohol Abuser

People who are struggling with alcohol need help, and you might be able to provide some. Place a plus sign (+) in the space to the left of the statement if the suggestion is a good one that is likely to help a drinker. Place a zero (0) in the space if the suggestion is not likely to be effective.

_____ 1. Organize an intervention.

_____ 2. Try to include the drinker in activities that do not involve alcohol.

_____ 3. Threaten or bribe the drinker when he or she has a relapse.

_____ 4. Provide the drinker with the names and phone numbers of organizations that help problem drinkers.

_____ 5. Argue with a drinker when he or she is drunk.

_____ 6. Let the drinker know that his or her drinking concerns you.

_____ 7. Do nothing. Allow the drinker to remain in denial about his or her problem for as long as he or she needs to.

_____ 8. Help the drinker feel good about quitting.

_____ 9. Emphasize the physical and psychological pain of withdrawal that the drinker will likely face.

_____ 10. Offer to drive the drinker home when he or she is intoxicated.

Provide the following definitions on the spaces provided.

11. Define the term *recovering alcoholic.*

_____

_____

12. Define the term *intervention.*

_____

_____

Chapter 12

Applying Heath Skills

Decision Making

Getting Someone Help

With a group, role-play a scene in which one or more teens decide how to help someone who may have an alcohol problem.

1. With the members of your group, think of two realistic situations in which teens must decide how to help someone who may have an alcohol problem. On separate index cards, write a brief description of each situation. These descriptions will be collected by your teacher and distributed to other groups to role-play for the class.

2. With your group, read and discuss the situation your teacher gives you. Write brief notes showing how one teen (or several teens) in that situation can use the decision-making steps to decide how to help someone who may have an alcohol problem.

   State the situation. _____

   _____

   List the options. _____

   _____

   Weigh the possible outcomes. _____

   _____

   _____

   Consider your values. _____

   _____

   Make a decision and act. _____

   _____

   Evaluate your decision. _____

   _____

3. Keeping the decision-making steps in mind, practice role-playing the situation your group has been given. Then perform your role-play for the class.

Chapter 12

Chapter 13 Study Guide
Tobacco

Study Tips

✔ Read the chapter objectives.

✔ Look up any unfamiliar words.

✔ Read the questions below before you read the chapter.

As you read the chapter, answer the following questions. Later you can use this guide to review the information in the chapter.

Lesson 1

1. What is tar, and how can it be harmful to the body?

_____

_____

_____

2. What is smokeless tobacco, and what are some of the negative effects it can have on the body?

_____

_____

_____

_____

Lesson 2

3. Name three short-term physical effects of tobacco use.

_____

_____

_____

_____

_____

_____

Chapter 13 Study Guide
Tobacco

4. What is cardiovascular disease?

_____

Lesson 3

5. What is a psychological dependence?

_____

_____

6. What are some of the psychological symptoms of nicotine withdrawal?

_____

_____

_____

Lesson 4

7. What is the difference between sidestream smoke and mainstream smoke?

_____

_____

8. What is a passive smoker?

_____

Lesson 6

9. What are point-of-sale promotions?

_____

_____

10. What are some ways you can stand up to negative peer pressure and avoid using tobacco products?

_____

_____

_____

Activity 44
Use with Chapter 13, Lesson 1

Tobacco Products

Match each of the words or terms on the left with its description on the right. Write the letter of the description in the space provided.

Bidis

Carbon monoxide

Addictive

Kreteks

Tobacco

Smokeless tobacco

Nicotine

Tar

1. Cigarettes containing sweet, candy-like flavorings

_____

2. A woody, shrub-like plant with large leaves

_____

3. A poisonous, colorless, odorless gas

_____

4. A thick, oily, dark liquid that forms when tobacco burns

_____

5. Causing intense cravings

_____

6. Ground tobacco that is chewed or inhaled through the nose

_____

7. Cigarettes that contain a mixture of tobacco, cloves, and other additives

_____

8. An addictive drug found in all tobacco products

9. What are the unhealthy effects of using smokeless tobacco?

_____

_____

_____

10. Imagine you have a friend who tells you that cigar smoking is not as dangerous as cigarette smoking because you do not inhale it into your lungs. What is your response?

_____

_____

_____

Activity 45
Use with Chapter 13, Lesson 2

Tobacco's Short-Term and Long-Term Effects

In the following statements, write whether the effect is a *short-term* or *long-term* effect of using tobacco. Fill in the blanks with terms from your textbook to complete the statements.

_____ 1. Tobacco use causes chemical changes to the _____.

_____ 2. Smoking is the leading cause of _____ cancer.

_____ 3. Tobacco stains the teeth and gums and increases the risk of gum

_____.

_____ 4. Smoking causes a dry, hacking _____, which is

a symptom of _____.

_____ 5. Smoking is a leading cause of cardiovascular disease, a disease of the

_____ and _____.

_____ 6. Smoking dulls the _____.

_____ 7. Smoking increases _____, such as asthma,

allergies, and bronchitis.

_____ 8. Smoking increases the user's _____ and blood

_____.

_____ 9. Smoking causes _____ of the bladder.

_____ 10. Smoking causes increased cholesterol _____.

Activity 46
Use with Chapter 13, Lesson 3

Questions About Tobacco Use

Answer the following questions about tobacco addiction.

1. What is the best way to keep from having a tobacco-related disease?

   _____

   _____

2. What kind of drug is nicotine?

   _____

3. What effect does this type of drug have on the body?

   _____

4. What are the warning signs that some people commonly experience
   when first using tobacco?

   _____

5. What happens once tolerance to tobacco occurs?

   _____

   _____

6. What is the difference between a physical dependence and a psychological dependence on nicotine?

   _____

   _____

   _____

7. Once psychological and physical dependencies are established, what
   is the tobacco user considered?

   _____

   _____

Activity 47
Use with Chapter 13, Lesson 4

Tobacco's Costs

Match the information from the column on the right with the information on the left to form a correct statement about the costs of tobacco to society. Write the letter in the space provided.

_____ **1.** For every dollar spent to spread the word about the dangers of smoking, tobacco companies spend _____ on marketing.

_____ **2.** The typical smoker spends _____ per day on tobacco.

_____ **3.** The average price per pack of cigarettes is up to _____.

_____ **4.** The average smoker spends about _____ per month on tobacco products.

_____ **5.** Each year tobacco companies spend _____ billion dollars on advertising.

_____ **6.** America's tobacco habit costs the nation nearly _____ billion dollars a year.

_____ **7.** Each year, the U.S. economy loses _____ billion dollars in productivity due to smoking.

_____ **8.** In 10 years' time, the average smoker will have spent _____ thousand dollars on tobacco.

a. $5

b. $23

c. $27

d. $240

e. $7.50

f. $225

g. $12.7

h. $80

Activity 49
Use With Chapter 13, Lesson 5

Chapter 13

Your Anti-Smoking Campaign

Imagine that you have been asked to design several bumper stickers that will inform others on the rights of the nonsmoker. Use as few words as possible to make your points.

Chapter 13 Health Inventory

The Truth About Tobacco

Some of these statements about tobacco are true and some are false.
Identify each statement by writing *true* or *false* in the space at the left.

_____ 1. The best way to remain tobacco-free is never to start using tobacco products.

_____ 2. Tobacco use has no effect on pubic health costs to the U.S. economy.

_____ 3. Tobacco use is not psychologically addictive.

_____ 4. Nonsmokers can be seriously harmed by secondhand smoke.

_____ 5. Cigar and pipe smokers do not run the risk of becoming addicted to nicotine.

_____ 6. Most smokers do not want to quit the habit.

_____ 7. Women who smoke during pregnancy risk premature delivery or having a low-birth-weight baby.

_____ 8. Several national associations sponsor programs that are designed to help people kick the tobacco habit.

_____ 9. Tobacco companies spend very little money on advertising, since the product "sells itself."

_____ 10. A small percentage of people who decide to quit smoking suffer a relapse within the first three months after quitting.

_____ 11. You have the right to breathe air that is free of tobacco smoke.

_____ 12. When tobacco smoke is inhaled, tar deposits form on the linings of the lungs.

Score yourself:

Write the number of *yes* answers here. ☐

Write the number of correct responses here:

10–12: Excellent

6–9: Fair

0–5: Reread Chapter 13 to learn the facts about tobacco use.

Chapter 14 Study Guide
Drugs

Study Tips

✔ Read the chapter objectives.

✔ Look up any unfamiliar words.

✔ Read the questions below before you read the chapter.

As you read the chapter, answer the following questions. Later you can use this guide to review the information in the chapter.

Lesson 1

1. What is the difference between prescription and over-the-counter medicines?

_____

_____

_____

_____

2. What is the difference between drug misuse and drug abuse?

_____

_____

_____

_____

_____

_____

Lesson 2

3. What are three short-term effects of marijuana use?

_____

_____

Chapter 14 Study Guide
Drugs

4. What are some of the negative effects of anabolic steroid use on teens?

_____

_____

_____

_____

Lesson 3

5. Name two narcotics that are commonly abused.

_____

_____

_____

_____

6. Name five of the most harmful effects of stimulant abuse.

_____

_____

_____

Lesson 4

7. Name two harmful effects of hallucinogens.

_____

_____

8. What damage do inhalants cause a user?

_____

_____

_____

_____

Chapter 14 Study Guide
Drugs

Lesson 5

9. What is the first step in getting help for drug abuse?

_____

_____

10. Name five treatment options for individuals needing help recovering from substance abuse.

_____

_____

_____

_____

Lesson 6

11. What is the S.T.O.P. strategy for refusing drugs?

_____

_____

12. What are six healthy alternatives to drug use?

_____

_____

_____

_____

_____

_____

Activity 50
Use with Chapter 14, Lesson 1

The Truth about Drug Abuse

Some of the statements below are facts and others are not. Classify each by writing *true* or *false* in the space at the left. On the lines that follow the statements, correct the ones you have identified as false.

_____ 1. Drug addiction is a disease.

_____

_____ 2. Taking more of a drug than a doctor prescribes is abuse.

_____

_____ 3. Side effects will not happen if you take medicines properly.

_____

_____ 4. A drug tolerance might develop if you take a medicine for a long period of time.

_____

_____ 5. Using legal drugs for non-medical reasons is drug abuse.

_____

_____ 6. Abusers often have trouble functioning without drugs.

_____

_____ 7. Combining over-the-counter medicines is perfectly safe.

_____

_____ 8. To safely dispose of outdated or unused pills, simply throw them away.

_____

_____ 9. Drug abuse can affect all three sides of your health triangle.

_____

_____ 10. An addiction means someone has a physical need for a drug.

_____

Activity 51
Use with Chapter 14, Lesson 2

Truth About Illegal Drugs

Some of the following statements about preventing violence are facts and others are not. Classify each statement by writing *true* or *false* in the space at the left. On the lines that follow the statements, correct the ones you have identified as false.

_____ **1.** Marijuana users are at risks for the same lung diseases that tobacco users face, including cancer.

_____

_____

_____ **2.** There are approximately 100 chemicals in marijuana.

_____

_____

_____ **3.** Amnesia is the main active chemical in marijuana.

_____

_____

_____ **4.** People react the same way to club drugs.

_____

_____

_____ **5.** Ecstasy, like marijuana, comes from a plant.

_____

_____

_____ **6.** GHB and Rohypnol have both been linked to sexual assault.

_____

_____

_____ **7.** Steroid use can cause a hormonal imbalance in teen users.

_____

_____

Activity 52
Use with Chapter 14, Lesson 3

Matching

Match the definitions in the left column with the appropriate term.
Write the letter in the space provided.

_____ 1. A drug that stimulates the central nervous system

_____ 2. When a drug is taken repeatedly at increasingly high doses

_____ 3. Liquid from the poppy plant containing substances that numb the body

_____ 4. Illegal stimulant derived from the coca plant

_____ 5. A feeling of well-being or elation

_____ 6. Used to treat patients with more serious anxiety and panic attacks

_____ 7. Drugs that speed up activity in the human brain and spinal cord

_____ 8. Substances that slow down normal brain function

a. Euphoria

b. Amphetamine

c. CNS depressants

d. Cocaine

e. Opium

f. Benzodiazepines

g. Binge

h. Stimulants

Answer the following questions about drugs. Write your answers on the lines provided.

9. How do narcotics work?

_____

_____

_____

10. What are the harmful effects of depressants?

_____

_____

_____

Activity 53
Use with Chapter 14, Lesson 4

Chapter 14

Understanding Hallucinogens and Inhalants

In the space, write the word from the list that will best complete each statement.

1. _____ is a drug made from lysergic acid.

2. A(n) _____ is any substance whose fumes are sniffed and inhaled to produce mind-altering sensations.

3. The _____ effects of LSD are often very difficult to predict.

4. _____ is not a true hallucinogen in its chemical makeup, but its effects are similar to the effects of other hallucinogens.

5. _____ are drugs that distort moods, thoughts, and senses.

6. If _____ is damaged, nerve cells may not be able to send messages to other parts of the body.

PCP

myelin

LSD

hallucinogens

inhalant

psychological

Answer the following questions about drug use. Write your answers on the lines provided.

7. What are some of the harmful effects of hallucinogens?

_____

_____

8. What are some of the warning signs of inhalant abuse?

_____

_____

9. What are some of the harmful effects of inhalants?

_____

_____

10. What damage do inhalants cause?

_____

_____

Activity 54

Recognizing the Symptoms

Drug addiction is treatable. The first step to getting help is admitting that a drug problem exists. Recognizing the symptoms is key. Place a plus sign (+) in the space to the left of the statement if it describes a symptom of a person likely using drugs. Place a zero (0) in the space if the statement is not necessarily a sign of drug abuse.

_____ 1. Dwayne always loved everything to do with baseball, including playing it, watching it, and collecting memorabilia. Yet, these days, his brother cannot convince him to even play catch.

_____ 2. Megan's grade in algebra dropped from an A to a C in one marking period.

_____ 3. Caitlyn's longtime friend confronts her to ask if she had a drug problem; Caitlyn laughs and denies it.

_____ 4. Jacob realizes he needs increasingly larger amounts of drugs to get high.

_____ 5. Jasmine is slowly losing weight.

_____ 6. Kirsten has dyed her hair black and begun dressing all in black.

_____ 7. Mike craves marijuana whenever his stepfather confronts him about grades.

_____ 8. Peter is bulking up bigger and faster than anyone else on the football team.

_____ 9. Sophie finds herself taking more drugs than she meant to, and using drugs at times and places she had not planned.

_____ 10. Will's mom notices that money and jewelry have begun to go missing since Will started hanging out with a new group of friends.

Provide the following definitions on the spaces provided.

11. Describe _tolerance_.

_____

12. Describe _withdrawal symptoms_.

_____

Activity 55

Say No to Drugs

Refusing to give in to peer pressure can be hard at times. Listed below are several ways to say no to drugs. Complete the remaining sentences by suggesting other ways to refuse drugs.

1. No thanks, drugs are illegal.

2. No thanks, I'm getting in shape.

3. No thanks, I don't like to be out of control.

4. No thanks, _____

5. No thanks, _____

6. No thanks, _____

7. No thanks, _____

8. No thanks, _____

9. No thanks, _____

10. No thanks, _____

11. No thanks, _____

12. No thanks, _____

13. No thanks, _____

14. No thanks, _____

15. No thanks, _____

16. No thanks, _____

17. No thanks, _____

18. No thanks, _____

19. No thanks, _____

20. No thanks!

Applying Health Skills

Analyzing Influences

Staying Drug Free

Think of the factors that have influenced you to be drug free. Create a jigsaw puzzle showing the factors.

1. Think about the factors that have influenced you to be drug free. List the five most important factors here.

_____

_____

_____

_____

_____

2. Choose an object that symbolizes one aspect of your personality. For example, if you enjoy art, you might choose an easel or a paint brush. Name the object you have chosen.

_____

3. On a sheet of light-colored construction paper, make a large outline drawing of the object you have chosen.

4. Cut out the object you have drawn. Then cut the object into five pieces to create a jigsaw puzzle. On each puzzle piece, write one of the factors you have listed above.

5. Switch puzzles with a classmate. Put your classmate's puzzle together, and glue the pieces onto a piece of poster board.

6. Display your completed puzzle in the classroom. Look at your classmates' completed puzzles. Use tally marks to record how many other students recorded the same important factors you listed.

Chapter 15 Study Guide
Personal Care and Consumer Choices

Study Tips
✔ Read the chapter objectives.
✔ Look up any unfamiliar words.
✔ Read the questions below before you read the chapter.

 As you read the chapter, answer the following questions. Later you can use this guide to review the information in the chapter.

Lesson 1

1. List the skin's basic functions.

_____

_____

2. Name three causes for skin problems.

_____

_____

3. Describe the parts of good tooth and gum care.

_____

_____

_____

Lesson 2

4. What is a consumer?

_____

5. Identify four factors that can influence a person's buying decisions.

_____

_____

_____

Chapter 15 Study Guide
Perssonal Care and Consumer Choices

Lesson 3

6. How do prescription medicines differ from nonprescription medicines?

_____

_____

_____

7. Define *side effect*.

_____

8. Name three risks of medicines.

_____

_____

_____

Lesson 4

9. Name three types of health care facilities available in most communities.

_____

_____

10. What is managed care?

_____

_____

Lesson 5

11. Name two health programs that are overseen by the Department of Health and Human Services.

_____

_____

_____

Chapter 15

Chapter 15 Study Guide
Perssonal Care and Consumer Choices

12. What is the job of the Consumer Product Safety Commission?

_____

_____

_____

_____

13. What international organizations have made world health a priority?

_____

_____

_____

Activity 56
Use with Chapter 15, Lesson 1

Skin, Teeth, Hair, and Nails

Imagine that you are on a quiz show and one of the categories is Personal Health Care. The quiz show host presents only the answers. You must supply the questions.

1. **Answer:** A physician who specializes in skin problems.

   Question: _____

2. **Answer:** The outermost layer of skin.

   Question: _____

3. **Answer:** A hole caused by an acid formed from sugar and plaque.

   Question: _____

4. **Answer:** The body's largest organ.

   Question: _____

5. **Answer:** A soft, colorless sticky film containing bacteria that coats your teeth.

   Question: _____

6. **Answer:** The eye's clear protective structure that lets light in.

   Question: _____

7. **Answer:** A measure of the loudness of sound.

   Question: _____

8. **Answer:** The tough substance composing hair and nails.

   Question: _____

9. **Answer:** Hearing loss.

   Question: _____

10. **Answer:** The thin layer of nerve cells that covers the interior back of the eye and absorbs light.

    Question: _____

Activity 57

Becoming a Skilled Consumer

Design package labels that appeal to teens for the variety of products below. Make sure to include all important product information that smart consumers might look for. Refer to package labels at home and at stores for ideas about ingredients, etc.

Toothpaste

Product name: _____

Amount in container: _____

Product's intended use: _____

Warnings: _____

Directions for use: _____

Ingredients: _____

Manufacturer's contact information: _____

Acne cream

Product name: _____

Amount in container: _____

Product's intended use: _____

Warnings: _____

Directions for use: _____

Ingredients: _____

Manufacturer's contact information: _____

Shampoo

Product name: _____

Amount in container: _____

Product's intended use: _____

Warnings: _____

Directions for use: _____

Ingredients: _____

Manufacturer's contact information: _____

Activity 58

Use with Chapter 15, Lesson 3

Take Your Medicine–Wisely!

Read each situation. Then answer the questions below.

Situation 1

Jessica's grandmother has a heart condition and lives in an assisted living facility with many other senior citizens. As winter approaches, the doctor urges her to protect herself against the flu. What type of medicine is used to prevent flu?

_____

Situation 2

Molly has a toothache. The dentist has no appointments open until tomorrow. What type of medicine might help Molly?

_____

Situation 3

Jared has a sore throat, and his doctor diagnosed it as strep. What medicine will help Jared?

_____

Situation 4

Sara took a pill this morning for her hay fever and it relieved her stuffy nose and itchy eyes, but by the time she's reached her first-period class, she feels very sleepy. Why?

_____

Situation 5

Matt's baby brother has a doctor's appointment and the doctor gives him a shot even though the infant is healthy and happy. What kind of medicine did the doctor administer and why?

_____

Situation 6

Cara twists her ankle during cheerleading practice. In addition to getting rest, Cara might consider taking what kind of medicine?

_____

Activity 59

Choosing a Specialist

Read each statement below. Then decide which health care specialist would be the best one to visit for treatment. Write the letter of the appropriate provider in the space at the left.

_____ 1. When B.J. had a physical before trying out for the football team, his doctor told him he had a heart murmur and advised him to see this specialist.

_____ 2. Jen's younger brother, who has leukemia, is under the care of this specialist.

_____ 3. Nadine has been sad for more than a month. She has lost interest in the activities she used to love and her grades are dropping. She feels hopeless.

_____ 4. Bryan wants to make the wrestling team and compete in a weight class that requires him to gain 10 pounds. His brother told him to eat lots of French fries and chocolate bars, but his father made him an appointment with this specialist.

_____ 5. Lisette's aunt, who has been diagnosed with breast cancer, is undergoing chemotherapy when she visits this specialist.

_____ 6. Ian's grandfather needs his pacemaker checked regularly by this specialist.

_____ 7. This specialist might find him or herself testifying in court about the sanity of an accused criminal.

_____ 8. Kelly suffers from severe headaches, so her mother made an appointment for her to see this specialist.

a. osteopath

b. oncologist

c. cardiologist

d. psychiatrist

e. dietitian

f. neurologist

Activity 60
Use with Chapter 15, Lesson 5

Public Health

Some of the statements below are true and others are not. Classify each by writing *true* or *false* in the space at the left. On the lines that follow the statements, correct the ones you have identified as false.

_____ 1. Every county in every state has its own public health department.

_____

_____ 2. At the federal level, public health is overseen by the National Institutes of Health.

_____

_____ 3. An announcement that informs the public that a product has been determined unsafe is a public service announcement.

_____

_____ 4. The Consumer Product Safety Commission works to reduce risks from unsafe products.

_____

_____ 5. The Department of Health and Human Services is responsible for the Medicare and Medicaid systems.

_____

_____ 6. The American Cancer Society is the world's premier medical research organization.

_____

_____ 7. In many places around the globe, populations are faced with famine.

_____

_____ 8. The World Health Organization is an agency of the United Nations.

_____

_____ 9. The Indian Health Service is one of the main agencies of the Department of Health and Human Services.

_____

_____ 10. The American Heart Association is paid for by tax dollars.

_____

Chapter 15 Health Inventory

Personal Care

Read the questions below. In the space at the left, write *yes* if the item describes you, or *no* if it does not describe you.

_____ **1.** I know my rights as a consumer.

_____ **2.** I compare products before I buy.

_____ **3.** I care about getting the best product for my money.

_____ **4.** I know where to get help for a consumer problem.

_____ **5.** I avoid being talked into purchases by salespeople.

_____ **6.** I am aware of external factors that can play a role in decision making.

_____ **7.** I look for products that offer a warranty.

_____ **8.** I keep receipts for products I have purchased.

_____ **9.** I know how to return an unsatisfactory or defective product.

_____ **10.** I have excellent consumer skills.

_____ **11.** I am able to analyze the influences on my buying practices.

_____ **12.** I have a good sense of my own personal taste.

_____ **13.** I am able to analyze advertisements on television.

_____ **14.** I read label ingredients before I buy a product.

_____ **15.** I know what to do in case of fraud.

Score yourself:

Write the number of *yes* answers here.

12–15: You are an alert consumer.

8–11: You're a fair consumer.

Fewer than 8: Buyers beware! Remember, it's your money and your health. Learn the facts.

Chapter 16 Study Guide
Your Body Systems

Study Tips

✔ Read the chapter objectives.

✔ Look up any unfamiliar words.

✔ Read the questions below before you read the chapter.

As you read the chapter, answer the following questions. Later you can use this guide to review the information in the chapter.

Lesson 1

1. How many bones are in the body?

_____

_____

2. Define the three types of connective tissue.

_____

_____

_____

_____

_____

Lesson 2

3. What are cardiac muscles?

_____

_____

_____

Lesson 3

4. What are the parts of blood?

_____

_____

Chapter 16

Chapter 16 Study Guide
Your Body Systems

5. What are capillaries?

_____

_____

_____

Lesson 4

6. What are the two parts to respiration?

_____

_____

_____

_____

_____

_____

7. What are some things you can do to help care for your respiratory system?

_____

_____

_____

_____

_____

Lesson 5

8. What are the two main parts of the nervous system, and what do they include?

_____

_____

_____

_____

_____

Chapter 16 Study Guide
Your Body Systems

9. What are the two parts of the peripheral nervous system? Define them.

_____

_____

_____

_____

_____

Lesson 6

10. What is digestion?

_____

_____

Lesson 7

11. What is the pituitary gland?

_____

_____

Lesson 8

12. What is menstruation, how long does it usually last, and how often does it usually occur?

_____

_____

_____

Chapter 16

Activity 61
Use with Chapter 16, Lesson 1

Your Skeletal System

From the list at the left, choose the type of joint found in the parts of the body listed on the right. Terms in the box may be used more than once. Then identify each type of skeletal system problem described at the bottom, using the terms listed in the box.

_____ **1.** Knees

_____ **2.** Collar Bone

_____ **3.** Shoulders

_____ **4.** Between the Neck and the Head

_____ **5.** Elbows

_____ **6.** Hips

_____ **7.** Ankles

Ball-and-socket
Gliding
Hinge
Pivot

_____ **8.** A disorder in which the spine curves to one side of the body

_____ **9.** A bone disorder most often seen in older adults in which the bones become brittle

_____ **10.** Occurs when a bone is pushed out of its joint

_____ **11.** A break in a bone

_____ **12.** An overuse injury common among runners and aggressive walkers

Scoliosis
Shin Splint
Osteoporosis
Fracture
Dislocation

Chapter 16

Activity 62
Use with Chapter 16, Lesson 2

The Muscular System

Using words and terms from your textbook, complete the following sentences.

1. Your muscular system is the group of structures that gives your body

   parts the power to _____.

2. The muscles attached to bones that enable you to move are called

   _____ muscles.

3. Your _____ muscles are found in organs, blood
   vessels, and glands.

4. Involuntary muscles found only in the walls of your heart are

   _____ muscles.

5. Muscle movement is triggered by _____.

6. Before exercising you should always _____ up.

7. The best way to keep your muscles toned is to _____

   well and keep _____.

8. When you lift something heavy, never _____
   over.

9. Sore muscles are a _____ condition.

10. Muscle strain is usually a result of _____ the
    muscle.

Chapter 16

Activity 63
Use with Chapter 16, Lesson 3

Your Circulatory System

Imagine that you have been asked to answer questions in a health class about the circulatory system because you are an expert in this area. Write your responses to these questions.

1. What is the circulatory system?

   _____

   _____

2. What is the difference between veins and arteries?

   _____

   _____

3. What is blood made up of?

   _____

   _____

4. What is the difference between white blood cells and red blood cells?

   _____

   _____

5. What is the job of platelets?

   _____

   _____

6. How can I keep my circulatory system healthy?

   _____

   _____

Activity 64
Use with Chapter 16, Lesson 4

Your Respiratory System

Imagine that you are on a quiz show. One of the categories is the human respiratory system. The quiz show host presents an answer. You have to write a question.

1. **Answer:** You would not be able to eat without having this flap of tissue that covers your trachea when you swallow.

   Question: _____

2. **Answer:** It's here that oxygen is transferred to the blood and carbon dioxide is removed.

   Question: _____

3. **Answer:** Microscopic air sacs in the lungs where carbon dioxide is exchanged with oxygen.

   Question: _____

4. **Answer:** This disease, in which alveoli are damaged or destroyed, causes serious breathing difficulties.

   Question: _____

5. **Answer:** They are respiratory problems that are strongly linked to smoking.

   Question: _____

6. **Answer:** This passage, also called the windpipe, directs air to the lungs.

   Question: _____

7. **Answer:** This is where air enters and leaves the body.

   Question: _____

8. **Answer:** This large dome-shaped muscle that separates the lungs from the abdomen.

   Question: _____

Activity 65
Use with Chapter 16, Lesson 5

Your Nervous System

Imagine that the parts of your nervous system can speak. In the space provided, identify each of the following parts of the nervous system by their descriptions.

_____ **1.** I am your body's message and control center.

_____ **2.** I am a system that includes the brain and the spinal cord.

_____ **3.** I am a system that includes nerves that get information from all parts of the body.

_____ **4.** I am a system dealing with actions that you control.

_____ **5.** I am a system that deals with actions you do not control.

_____ **6.** I am a condition caused by the brain being jarred and striking the inside of the skull.

_____ **7.** I am a column of nerve tissue about 18 inches long.

_____ **8.** I am the bones that make up your spine.

_____ **9.** I am specialized nerve cells that send and receive impulses.

_____ **10.** I am the connective membranes in the spine.

Chapter 16

Activity 66

Use with Chapter 16, Lesson 6

Caring for Your Digestive System

Below are guidelines for caring for your digestive system. Read the **DO list** to find out what you should do to care for your digestive system. **Read the DON'T list to learn what to avoid.**

DO
- Eat slowly
- Chew your food thoroughly
- Eat fiber-rich foods
- Drink eight 8-ounce glasses of water a day
- Get regular dental checkups
- Practice good oral hygiene

DON'T
- Forget to drink eight 8-ounce glasses of water a day
- Skip meals
- Rush through a meal
- Forget to chew food thoroughly
- Eat foods low in fiber

During the next three days, try to practice the Do's listed above and avoid the Don'ts. Monitor yourself three times a day—morning, afternoon, and evening. Use the chart below to show your progress. Write an *O* in the chart for each Do you practice during that part of the day. Write an *X* for each Don't.

	Day 1	Day 2	Day 3
Morning			
Afternoon			
Evening			

At the end of the three days, add the total number of Os and Xs. Write these numbers below.

Number of *O*s _____   Number of *X*s _____

If there are more *O*s than *X*s, give yourself a reward. If there are more *X*s than *O*s, list three ways you can improve the care of your digestive system.

_____

_____

_____

Chapter 16

Activity 67

Use with Chapter 16, Lesson 7

Your Endocrine System

Read each statement about the endocrine system. If the statement is true, write + on the line provided. If the statement is false, write 0 in the space provided and then rewrite the statement to make it true.

_____ 1. A gland is a group of cells or an organ that secretes a *substance*.

_____

_____ 2. The endocrine glands operate based on signals from the *heart*.

_____

_____ 3. The most common problem of the endocrine system is *diabetes*.

_____

_____ 4. The chemicals secreted by the endocrine glands are called *pituitaries*.

_____

_____ 5. Most cases of diabetes are *type 1*.

_____

_____ 6. Regular physical activity and good nutrition help *endocrine health*.

_____

_____ 7. Tiredness and depression are symptoms of *underactive* thyroids.

_____

_____ 8. The endocrine glands are located in *one part of the body*.

_____

_____ 9. The adrenals, ovaries, and testes are all glands of the *endocrine* system.

_____

_____ 10. People with underactive thyroids may experience weight *loss*.

_____

Activity 68
Use with Chapter 16, Lesson 8

Your Reproductive System

Match each definition in the left column with the correct term from the right column. Write the letter of the term in the space provided.

_____ 1. Process by which one mature egg is released each month

_____ 2. When the lining of the uterus, an unfertilized egg, and some blood flow out of the body

_____ 3. Organ that receives and nourishes a fertilized egg

_____ 4. Occurs when an internal organ pushes against or through a surrounding cavity wall.

_____ 5. When a male sperm cell joins with a female egg cell

_____ 6. The male reproductive glands

_____ 7. Forceful muscular contractions during which semen exits the penis

_____ 8. Hormonal changes that occur in females from the beginning of one menstruation to the next

_____ 9. The persistent inability to get pregnant

_____ 10. The mixture of fluids and sperm

a. Ejaculation

b. Ovulation

c. Fertilization

d. Menstrual cycle

e. Infertility

f. Hernia

g. Testes

h. Menstruation

i. Semen

j. Uterus

Chapter 16

Applying Health Skills

Accessing Information

Body Systems

In this chapter you have learned about the systems of the body. Research and prepare a fact sheet on a specific body system or part of a body system.

1. Choose a body system or part of a body system that you would like to learn more about. For example, if you have a friend with diabetes, you might want to learn more about the endocrine system. Name the body system or body system part that you have chosen.

_____

2. Read about that body system or body system part in reliable print and/or Internet sources. On the lines below, record at least three facts you did not know before you began your research. Note the source where you found each fact.

_____

_____

_____

_____

_____

_____

_____

_____

_____

Chapter 16

Chapter 17 Study Guide
Growth and Development

Study Tips
✔ Read the chapter objectives.
✔ Look up any unfamiliar words.
✔ Read the questions below before you read the chapter.

As you read the chapter, answer the following questions. Later you can use this guide to review the information in the chapter.

Lesson 1

1. What is fertilization?

_____

_____

_____

2. What is the uterus?

_____

_____

_____

3. What occurs in stages two and three of the birth process?

_____

_____

_____

_____

_____

_____

_____

Chapter 17

Chapter 17 Study Guide
Growth and Development

Lesson 2

4. What is a genetic disorder? Name two examples of genetic disorders.

_____

_____

_____

_____

_____

_____

_____

5. What is prenatal care?

_____

_____

_____

6. How can alcohol use during pregnancy lead to birth defects?

_____

_____

_____

_____

_____

Lesson 3

7. What are the eight stages of development?

_____

_____

_____

_____

_____

_____

Chapter 17

Chapter 17 Study Guide
Growth and Development

8. What occurs in the middle childhood stage of childhood?

_____

_____

_____

_____

_____

9. What are some of the physical changes female adolescents experience?

_____

_____

_____

_____

_____

Lesson 4

10. What are some things people do in middle adulthood?

_____

_____

_____

_____

11. What are some things people do in late adulthood?

_____

_____

_____

_____

_____

12. What is the difference between chronological age and social age?

_____

_____

Chapter 17

Activity 69
Use with Chapter 17, Lesson 1

New Life

Write the correct title from the list below on each numbered answer line. Then arrange the steps in each lettered list in the correct order.

Titles:

The Birth Process

Fertilization and Early Growth

Fetal Development

1. _____

_____ **a.** The fertilized cluster of cells attaches itself to the wall of the uterus.

_____ **b.** The placenta begins to provide nourishment to the developing fetus.

_____ **c.** The fertilized cell begins to divide.

_____ **d.** A sperm cell joins with an egg cell.

2. _____

_____ **a.** The heart, brain, and lungs begin to form.

_____ **b.** The arms and legs can move freely.

_____ **c.** The heart is beating.

_____ **d.** Body organs have developed to function on their own.

3. _____

_____ **a.** Contractions push the placenta out of the mother's body.

_____ **b.** Mild contractions begin.

_____ **c.** The cervix opens to a width of about 4 inches.

_____ **d.** The baby is born.

Chapter 17

Activity 70
Use with Chapter 17, Lesson 2

Heredity and Environment

Imagine that you are on a quiz show. One of the categories is "Heredity and Environment." The quiz show host presents an answer. You have to write a question.

1. **Answer:** These threadlike structures are found within the nucleus of a cell that carry the codes for inherited traits.

   Question: _____

2. **Answer:** This is the sum total of a person's surroundings.

   Question: _____

3. **Answer:** During a prenatal visit, a woman's doctor may use this technology, which uses sound waves to form a picture of the fetus.

   Question: _____

4. **Answer:** These are abnormalities present at birth that cause physical or mental disability or death.

   Question: _____

5. **Answer:** This is a doctor whose specialty is the care of pregnant women and their fetuses.

   Question: _____

6. **Answer:** This occurs in a baby when the baby's genes supplied by one or both parents are abnormal or changed in some way.

   Question: _____

7. **Answer:** These are physical characteristics, such as eye color, hair color, or body shape passed on from parents to their children.

   Question: _____

8. **Answer:** These are the basic units of heredity.

   Question: _____

Chapter 17

Activity 71

The Stages of Growth

Even though everyone grows at a slightly different rate, each individual passes through certain stages of development. Read the description of each person below. Identify the developmental stage by writing *I* for infancy, *E* for early childhood, *M* for middle childhood, *L* for late childhood, or *A* for adolescence.

_____ 1. Brendan has just learned to climb stairs. He feels proud of his accomplishment but does not understand why his mother was upset when she saw him climbing the stairs in their home by himself.

_____ 2. Hannah would rather run than walk. She loves to pretend she is a monster that growls and chases people. She is very curious about the world around her and constantly asks her parents, "Why?" about everything she sees.

_____ 3. Toshio is beginning to recognize the people around him. He smiles when he sees his mother's face and laughs when he is tickled. He wants to touch everything he can reach.

_____ 4. Andre has recently developed a great interest in jigsaw puzzles. After many tries, he has successfully put together his first large puzzle all by himself.

_____ 5. Cory is beginning to develop a sense of his own identity. He is often irritated for no reason and has grown several inches in the last year.

_____ 6. Jamal has started following his father around the house and imitating what he does. He wants to help him with everything, so his father bought him a play set of tools to use while he works on his own projects.

_____ 7. Kendra has recently added several new words to her vocabulary, but her favorite word is still no. She is able to ask for what she wants now, using one to three words at a time.

_____ 8. In the last few weeks, Sierra has made several new friends. They sit together at the lunch table and play handball at recess.

_____ 9. Stephen is teased by his family for his cracking, changing voice, and he thinks it is funny too. He has applied for a part-time job after school, and is looking forward to more independence.

Chapter 17

Activity 72

Use with Chapter 17, Lesson 4

Growing Older and Staying Well

After we become adults, we pass through three basic stages in the aging process: early adulthood, middle adulthood, and late adulthood. Each stage is marked by certain milestones, and how well we age depends on a variety of physical, mental and emotional, and physical factors.

Complete the charts below by identifying some of these milestones and factors. Then answer the questions that follow.

Stage of Adulthood	Milestones
Early Adulthood	
Middle Adulthood	
Late Adulthood	

Health Triangle	Factors that can affect aging
Physical Health	
Mental/Emotional Health	
Social Health	

1. What are three different ways in which age can be measured?

   _____

   _____

2. Why is it important for adults to pay attention to all three sides of the health triangle?

   _____

   _____

Chapter 17 Health Inventory

Becoming an Adult

Read the statements below. In the space at the left, write *yes* if the statement describes you, or *no* if it does not describe you.

_____ 1. I think that my chances of reaching my goals for the future are good.

_____ 2. I am now preparing for the responsibilities and challenges of adulthood.

_____ 3. I expect to work for what I want rather than just have things happen to me.

_____ 4. I think it is important to be involved in the community even though I am still in my teen years.

_____ 5. I am good at accepting changes in my life.

_____ 6. I am beginning to think about the type of work I am interested in doing after I finish high school.

_____ 7. I get my school assignments completed on time.

_____ 8. I can make my own decisions without giving in to peer pressure.

_____ 9. I carry out my responsibilities without being reminded.

_____ 10. I know what people like and dislike about me.

_____ 11. I expect to be mentally and physically active throughout my life.

_____ 12. My behavior reflects my personal standards and values.

_____ 13. I believe that good health is important to the aging process.

_____ 14. Staying mentally active is just as important as staying physically active.

_____ 15. I intend to stick with the healthy eating and exercise habits that I am developing in my teen years.

Score yourself:

Write the number of *yes* answers here.

12–15: Excellent

8–11: Good

Fewer than 8: Adolescence is a time to begin taking more responsibility for your actions. How can you improve in this area?

Chapter 17

Chapter 18 Study Guide
Communicable Diseases

Study Tips
✔ Read the chapter objectives.
✔ Look up any unfamiliar words.
✔ Read the questions below before you read the chapter.

As you read the chapter, answer the following questions. Later you can use this guide to review the information in the chapter.

Lesson 1

1. What are four common types of pathogens?

_____

_____

_____

2. Name four ways pathogens spread.

_____

_____

_____

_____

Lesson 2

3. What is the function of the immune system?

_____

_____

_____

_____

4. What is the lymphatic system?

_____

_____

Chapter 18

Chapter 18 Study Guide
Communicable Diseases

Lesson 3

5. How are the cold and the flu similar and different?

_____

_____

_____

_____

6. How is hepatitis spread?

_____

_____

_____

_____

Lesson 4

7. What are sexually transmitted diseases sometimes called?

_____

8. What are three sexually transmitted diseases caused by bacteria?

_____

_____

_____

9. What is the best way to avoid getting a sexually transmitted disease?

_____

_____

_____

Lesson 5

10. What is a carrier?

_____

_____

_____

Chapter 18 Study Guide
Communicable Diseases

11. How is HIV spread?

_____

_____

_____

_____

12. What are three ways HIV infection and AIDS can be prevented?

_____

_____

_____

Chapter 18

Activity 73

Preventing Communicable Diseases

There are various ways to prevent the spread of communicable diseases. Read the following situations. Write the unhealthy behavior in each situation below. Then write the healthful behavior that will help defend against disease.

Situation 1
Dylan's brother, Thomas, has had a bad cold for the last week. Dylan made a sandwich for lunch while Thomas sat at the table eating a bowl of soup. "Can I have some of your soup?" Dylan asked.

_____

_____

Situation 2
Nicole had the flu for two days. After the second day at home, she did not feel much better, but refused to be home another day. A big test was approaching and Nicole wanted to be sure she would be there for the review. She asked her father to cancel the doctor's appointment he made and got ready to go to school.

_____

_____

Situation 3
At the neighborhood barbeque, Shakira could not wait to have a hamburger off the grill. When she took a large bite, she realized the inside of the burger was still very red and not warm. However, Shakira was so hungry she decided to keep eating.

_____

_____

Situation 4
Annie and Michael were walking home on a hot August day. They were both wearing shorts and t-shirts, but couldn't seem to cool off. Michael suggested they take a shortcut through the shaded forest because the woods were much cooler than the sidewalk. The woods were very dense and overgrown, but Annie agreed.

_____

_____

Chapter 18

Activity 74
Use with Chapter 18, Lesson 2

The Body's Defenses Against Infection

The body has three levels of defense against possible invading pathogens. Complete the following chart to show these levels of defense.

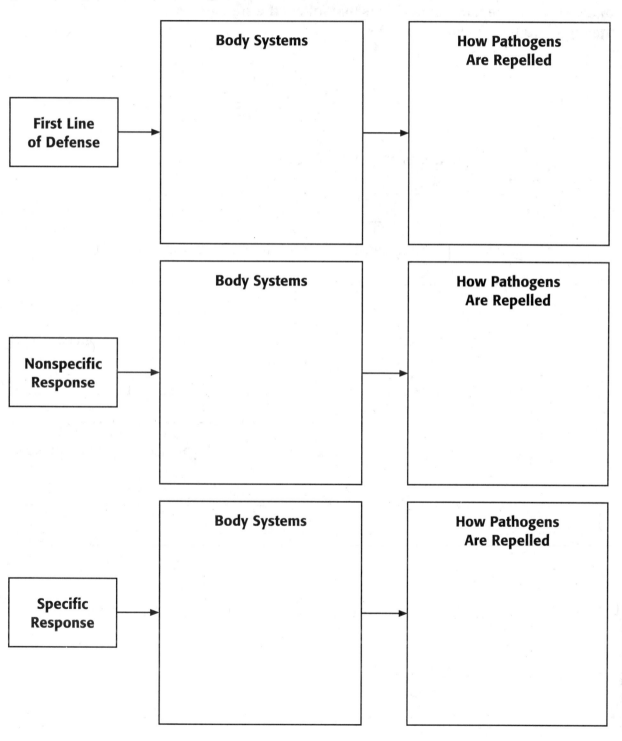

Activity 75

Use with Chapter 18, Lesson 3

Communicable Diseases

Some of the following statements about communicable diseases are facts and others are not. Classify each statement by writing *true* or *false* in the space at the left. One the lines that follow the statements, correct the ones you have identified as false.

_____ 1. The flu can only be spread through direct contact.

_____

_____

_____ 2. Only certain communicable diseases have a contagious period.

_____

_____

_____ 3. Chicken pox, measles, and mumps all have specific contagious periods.

_____

_____

_____ 4. Hepatitis, also known as "the kissing disease," is spread through contact with the saliva of an infected person.

_____

_____

_____ 5. Hepatitis A is most commonly spread through contact with contaminated blood or other body fluids.

_____

_____

_____ 6. Since tuberculosis can spread easily though the air, people are tested periodically to see if they have the disease.

_____

_____

_____ 7. Pneumonia and strep throat are both caused by bacteria and can be treated with antibiotics.

_____

_____

Chapter 18

Activity 76
Use with Chapter 18, Lesson 4

Understanding Sexually Transmitted Diseases

In the space, write the word(s) from the list that will best complete each statement.

1. Most STDs are spread only through _____ contact.

2. STDs can _____ because the body does not build up an immunity to them.

3. _____ can be passed on to another person even when the blisters are not present.

4. If _____ is left untreated, it can infect other parts of the body, such as the heart, and cause fertility problems for men and women.

5. Like Genital Herpes and Chlamydia, _____ is often a silent disease.

6. During the advanced stage, _____ can cause mental disorders, blindness, heart problems, paralysis, and even death.

Gonorrhea

Genital Herpes

HPV

Sexual

Syphilis

Recur

Answer the following questions about sexually transmitted diseases. Write your answers on the lines provided.

7. Can you tell if someone has an STD by his or her appearance?

_____

8. What is the difference between genital herpes and genital warts?

_____

_____

9. What is the best way to avoid getting an STD?

_____

_____

10. What can you do to spread awareness of STDs?

_____

_____

Chapter 18

Activity 77
Use with Chapter 18, Lesson 5

HIV/AIDS Facts and Myths

Some of the statements below are facts and others are not. Classify each by writing *fact* or *myth* on the line at the left.

_____ 1. One way to get HIV is to give blood.

_____ 2. Pricking the skin with contaminated needles can spread HIV.

_____ 3. People can catch HIV from infected insects.

_____ 4. Being infected with HIV makes it possible for other pathogens to attack the body.

_____ 5. Hugging someone who is infected with HIV can spread the disease.

_____ 6. AIDS does not have a cure.

_____ 7. HIV attacks and weakens the body's immune system.

_____ 8. Unborn babies can get HIV from their mothers.

_____ 9. One way to get HIV is to touch something an infected person has touched.

_____ 10. You can get HIV by swimming in the same pool as an infected person.

_____ 11. Tattoos and body piercings can spread HIV if performed with contaminated needles.

_____ 12. Those infected with HIV can spread HIV even though they show no signs of the virus themselves.

13. **Imagine you are in charge of informing the public about HIV/AIDS. On the lines below, list three ways you could get the facts to the public.**

_____

_____

_____

_____

_____

_____

Chapter 18

Name _____ Date _____ Class Period _____

Applying Health Skills

Practicing Healthful Behaviors

Preventing the Spread of Disease

With other students, create and perform a skit about ways to prevent the spread of pathogens.

1. With your partner or group, list at least five ways to prevent the spread of pathogens.

_____

_____

_____

_____

_____

2. Plan a short skit in which the characters discuss or demonstrate ways to prevent the spread of pathogens. Use the ideas you have listed above. Write a brief description of the situation, the characters, and the action of your skit.

_____

_____

_____

_____

_____

3. Together, practice acting out your skit.

4. Perform your skit for the rest of the class.

Chapter 18

Chapter 19 Study Guide
Noncommunicable Diseases

> ## Study Tips
> ✔ Read the chapter objectives.
> ✔ Look up any unfamiliar words.
> ✔ Read the questions below before you read the chapter.

As you read the chapter, answer the following questions. Later you can use this guide to review the information in the chapter.

Lesson 1

1. What are *congenital disorders*?

_____

_____

2. Name four risk factors for disease that you cannot control.

_____

_____

Lesson 2

3. What is the most common form of cancer?

_____

4. Define *carcinogens*.

_____

5. What are the ABCDs when looking for a change in a mole or other skin formation?

_____

_____

Chapter 19 Study Guide
Noncommunicable Diseases

Lesson 3

6. What is the difference between arteriosclerosis and atherosclerosis?

_____

_____

_____

7. How can being physically active help prevent heart disease?

_____

_____

8. What is bypass surgery?

_____

_____

_____

Lesson 4

9. What health concerns can be caused by diabetes?

_____

_____

10. How can physical activity and rest reduce the symptoms of arthritis?

_____

_____

11. What is an allergy?

_____

_____

12. Name three common triggers for asthma.

_____

_____

_____

Activity 78
Use with Chapter 19, Lesson 1

The Truth About Noncommunicable Diseases

Some of the following statements about noncommunicable diseases are facts and others are not. Classify each statement by writing *true* or *false* in the space at the left. On the lines that follow the statements, correct the ones you have identified as false.

_____ 1. Multiple sclerosis is an example of a degenerative disease.

_____

_____

_____ 2. All disorders that are present when the baby is born are called degenerative disorders.

_____

_____

_____ 3. The causes of most birth defects are known.

_____

_____

_____ 4. Chronic diseases are present either continuously or on and off over a long period of time.

_____

_____

_____ 5. While it is hard to determine who will develop a disease, researchers have found that behavior does not affect a person's chance of developing a disease.

_____

_____

_____ 6. Smog is one environmental factor that can cause respiratory disease.

_____

_____

Activity 79

Use with Chapter 19, Lesson 2

Understanding Cancer

Each patient described below is being treated for cancer. In each case, write the missing term in the space to the left of the case study.

Surgery	Remission	Recurrence
Chemotherapy	Biopsy	Radiation therapy

1. Patient A is undergoing _____, a treatment that uses X-rays or other forms of radiation to kill cancer cells.

2. Doctors have discovered a suspicious lump on Patient B and have decided to perform a _____ on the tissue.

3. _____ helped Patient C fight cancers that had already spread through the body.

4. Patient D's cancer treatment has been very successful. The doctors tell her the cancer is in _____.

5. Even though Patient E's cancer was in remission, a _____ has occurred.

6. The cancer in patient F has not spread to new parts of the body and has remained in one place. Doctors think _____ will be most effective in removing the cancerous cells from the body.

Do you know how to reduce the risk of cancer? Next to each factor, write a plus (+) sign if it can help keep your body healthy. Write a minus (–) sign if it does not reduce the risk of cancer.

_____ 7. Cigarette smoking

_____ 8. Limiting sun exposure

_____ 9. Eat a high intake of saturated fats

_____ 10. Performing self-examinations

_____ 11. Regular physical activity

Activity 80
Use with Chapter 19, Lesson 3

Heart and Circulatory Problems

Some of the following statements about heart and circulatory problems are facts and others are not. Classify each statement by writing *true* or *false* in the space at the left. On the lines that follow the statements, correct the ones you have identified as false.

_____ 1. Arteriosclerosis is a condition in which the pressure of the blood on the walls of the blood vessels stays at a level that is higher than normal.

_____

_____

_____ 2. If the space in the coronary arteries narrows, the limited space can stop the heart from getting enough oxygen.

_____

_____

_____ 3. High blood pressure can cause a heart attack or stroke.

_____

_____

_____ 4. A heart attack is a serious condition that occurs when an artery of the brain breaks or becomes blocked.

_____

_____

_____ 5. Smoking cigarettes can help you prevent heart disease, heart attacks, hypertension, and strokes.

_____

_____

_____ 6. An angioplasty is a way to open arteries that become blocked.

_____

_____

Activity 81

Use with Chapter 19, Lesson 4

Diabetes and Arthritis

Identify each term in the column on the right by matching it with the correct description in the column on the left. Write the letter of the term in the space provided.

_____ 1. A chronic disease characterized by pain, inflammation, swelling, and stiffness of the joints.

_____ 2. A condition in which the body cannot effectively use the insulin it produces.

_____ 3. A protein made in the pancreas that regulates the level of glucose in the blood

_____ 4. A disease that prevents the body from converting food into energy

_____ 5. A chronic disease that results from a breakdown in cartilage in the joints

_____ 6. A condition in which the immune system attacks insulin-producing cells in the pancreas

_____ 7. A disease of the joints marked by painful swelling and stiffness

Type 2 Diabetes

Osteoarthritis

Diabetes

Arthritis

Insulin

Rheumatoid Arthritis

Type 1 Diabetes

Answer the following questions about diabetes and arthritis. Write your answers on the lines provided.

8. Explain the difference between Type 1 and Type 2 diabetes in relation to insulin.

_____

_____

9. What are some ways to manage arthritis?

_____

_____

Activity 82
Use with Chapter 19, Lesson 5

Allergies and Asthma

Fill in the chart by listing six common allergens and one common source for that allergen.

Allergen	Common Sources for Allergen
1.	
2.	
3.	
4.	
5.	
6.	

7. Define *hives*.

_____

8. What are three basic tips for managing allergies?

_____

_____

_____

9. What happens during an asthma attack?

_____

_____

_____

_____

10. What are three strategies people with asthma can use to help avoid asthma attacks?

_____

_____

_____

_____

Chapter 19 Health Inventory

Prevention and Your Health

Do you follow the good health habits that will help protect you from getting noncommunicable diseases? Use the questions below to find out. Write *yes* or *no* in the space at the left of each statement.

_____ 1. Do you know your family's medical history?

_____ 2. Do you watch for the seven warning signs of cancer?

_____ 3. Do you limit the amount of fat you eat?

_____ 4. Do you perform regular self-examinations for breast or testicular cancer?

_____ 5. Do you limit the amount of salt you eat?

_____ 6. Do you use sunscreen to protect your skin from the sun?

_____ 7. Do you eat plenty of whole grains, fruits, and vegetables every day?

_____ 8. Do you know the warning signs of melanoma?

_____ 9. Do you avoid using drugs?

_____ 10. Do you maintain a healthy weight?

_____ 11. Do you avoid using tobacco products?

_____ 12. Do you engage in regular physical activity?

_____ 13. Do you get 8 to 9 hours of sleep each night?

_____ 14. Do you deal with stress in a healthy way?

_____ 15. Do you avoid using alcohol?

Score yourself:

Write the number of *yes* answers here. [   ]

12–15: Good for you! You are taking good care of yourself!

8–11: Fair. You can do better!

Fewer than 8: Remember only a healthy body can fight disease. Review Chapter 19 again to learn about the ways you can prevent diseases.

Chapter 20 Study Guide
Safety and Emergencies

> ## Study Tips
> ✔ Read the chapter objectives.
> ✔ Look up any unfamiliar words.
> ✔ Read the questions below before you read the chapter.

As you read the chapter, answer the following questions. Later you can use this guide to review the information in the chapter.

Lesson 1

1. What are some ways you can prevent electric shock at home?

_____

_____

_____

_____

2. What are some safety precautions for keeping guns in the home?

_____

_____

_____

_____

Lesson 2

3. What are some ways to stay safe when you ride a bike?

_____

_____

_____

_____

Chapter 20 Study Guide
Safety and Emergencies

4. What are some water safety rules you should follow to prevent drowning?

_____

_____

_____

_____

_____

_____

Lesson 3

5. What is a tornado?

_____

_____

6. What is a blizzard?

_____

_____

Lesson 4

7. Define *universal precautions.*

_____

_____

_____

8. What are some ways you can prepare yourself for an emergency?

_____

_____

_____

_____

_____

Chapter 20 Study Guide
Safety and Emergencies

Chapter 20

Lesson 5

9. What are some ways you can help a person who faints?

_____

_____

_____

_____

_____

10. What are heat cramps, and how should they be treated?

_____

_____

_____

_____

Lesson 6

11. What are abdominal thrusts?

_____

_____

_____

12. What are some things that can cause a person to go into shock?

_____

_____

_____

Activity 83
Use with Chapter 20, Lesson 1

Being Safety Conscious

Read the statements below. Write *safe* on the line at the left if the statement describes a safety-conscious person. Write *unsafe* if the statement describes a person who is not safety conscious. Change each unsafe behavior to a safe one on the line following the statement.

_____ 1. Jacob stores a loaded gun in his unlocked closet.

_____

_____ 2. Natalie tries to call attention to herself by taking unnecessary risks.

_____

_____ 3. Felicia's family practices fire drills regularly.

_____

_____ 4. Taylor sometimes acts recklessly to impress her peers.

_____

_____ 5. Will knows he has to be most careful when he is tired or upset.

_____

_____ 6. Jorge is always aware of his surroundings and of possible hazards.

_____

_____ 7. Fiona uses a step stool or a ladder when trying to reach high places.

_____

_____ 8. Morgan often acts on impulse instead of planning ahead.

_____

_____ 9. Jeremy almost never cleans his stove, even when he spills food on it.

_____

_____ 10. David takes responsibility for his own safety.

_____

Chapter 20

Activity 84
Use with Chapter 20, Lesson 2

Chapter 20

Staying Safe on the Road and Outdoors

Read the statements below. Identify each safe statement by writing *S* in the space at the left, and each unsafe statement by writing *U*.

_____ 1. Tori is shivering in the cold rain, but she decides to continue jogging for another hour.

_____ 2. Nicholas always uses his safety belt when he drives in a car.

_____ 3. Kaya dresses for a cold day outside by wearing several layers of clothing.

_____ 4. Emma and Thane agree to stay together during their hike up Willow Mountain.

_____ 5. Maeve often rides a bicycle on the road at night without wearing reflective clothing or having reflectors on her bike.

_____ 6. Although a thunderstorm is starting and he can see lightning in the distance, Ryan continues swimming in the lake.

_____ 7. Before the rest of Anna's family gets up each morning, she exercises alone by swimming across Raven Lake.

_____ 8. Brian hears someone calling for help from the deep end of the pool, so he jumps in to help even though he is not a strong swimmer.

_____ 9. Cody and Jared dare each other to eat the berries of the plants they find along their hiking trail.

_____ 10. Shoshana always wears a helmet when she rides her bike, even if she is just riding around the block near her house.

_____ 11. Before Terrel dives into the pool, he checks the depth of the water.

_____ 12. Although Alicia has been skiing only once, she agrees to try the expert slope with two of her friends, both of whom are advanced skiers.

_____ 13. Abbey ignores the "Thin Ice" warning signs because she wants to practice her ice skating routine for the upcoming competition.

_____ 14. Elvis refuses to wear a helmet when he skateboards because he says it interferes with his vision.

_____ 15. If Azar is in a hurry, he crosses in the middle of the city street instead of the crosswalk.

Activity 85

Use with Chapter 20, Lesson 3

Weather Emergencies

On the lines provided, tell what you would do in each weather emergency described below.

1. You are at home, listening to the radio, when a tornado warning is announced. What would you do?

_____

_____

_____

2. The National Weather Service has issued a hurricane warning for your area. You are the only person at home, and you have been unable to reach other family members by telephone. What would you do?

_____

_____

3. You are outdoors when a winter storm unexpectedly turns into a blizzard. What would you do?

_____

_____

_____

4. While walking home during a heavy rainstorm, you come to a stream that you usually walk across because it has stepping stones. However, the water is rising rapidly, and the current is much stronger than usual. What would you do?

_____

_____

5. Your house begins to shake, and you realize that an earthquake is taking place. What would you do?

_____

_____

_____

Chapter 20

Activity 86

Basic First Aid

Answer the following questions about basic first aid.

1. What is first aid?

_____

_____

2. Why is it important to know basic first aid?

_____

_____

3. What are universal precautions?

_____

_____

4. What are the four steps to take for most emergencies?

_____

_____

5. When dialing 911 for an emergency, what should you remember to do?

_____

_____

_____

Activity 87
Use with Chapter 20, Lesson 5

Common Emergencies

You can effectively help someone who is hurt if you know how to give first aid in common emergencies. Read the list for each common emergency below. Check your knowledge by writing *X* on the line in front of each item that tells what you should do.

Sprains

_____ 1. Move the injured part to keep it from becoming stiff.

_____ 2. Apply ice to reduce swelling and pain.

_____ 3. Elevate the sprained part above the level of the heart.

First-Degree Burns

_____ 4. Immerse the burned area in cold water, or apply cold compresses.

_____ 5. Remove loose skin.

_____ 6. Cover the burn with a sterile bandage.

Foreign Object in the Eye

_____ 7. Lightly touch the object with a moistened cotton swab.

_____ 8. Try to flush the object from the eye with clean water.

_____ 9. Rub the eye vigorously.

Nosebleeds

_____ 10. Have the person put his or her head down.

_____ 11. Pinch the nose for 5 to 10 minutes.

_____ 12. If bleeding continues, get medical help.

Insect Bites

_____ 13. Wash the affected area.

_____ 14. Apply a special lotion for bites.

_____ 15. Leave the bite uncovered.

Poisoning

_____ 16. Call the nearest poison control center.

_____ 17. Induce vomiting in all cases.

_____ 18. Be ready to provide information about the victim and the suspected poison.

Activity 88

Dealing with Life-Threatening Emergencies

Listed below are the steps that should be taken in certain life-threatening emergencies. Put the steps in the order in which they should be done by writing the correct letter in the space to the left. The first one in each group has been done for you.

Saving a Choking Adult

_____ **1.** Quickly thrust inward and upward, as if trying to lift the person.

_____ **2.** Repeat thrusts until the food or object is dislodged.

__a__ **3.** Stand behind the person and wrap your arms around his or her waist.

_____ **4.** Make a fist with one hand, and place it just above the person's navel.

Treating a Person in Shock

_____ **5.** Have the person lie down and raise the feet higher than the head.

_____ **6.** Look for signs of shock, such as a weak, rapid pulse and shallow breathing.

_____ **7.** Cover the person with a blanket or coat to keep him or her warm.

__a__ **8.** Loosen tight fitting clothing.

Stopping Severe Bleeding

_____ **9.** Apply direct pressure to the wound, using a clean cloth.

_____ **10.** Apply pressure to the artery that supplies the blood to the area of the wound.

_____ **11.** Raise the site of bleeding above the level of the heart.

__a__ **12.** Have the person lie down.

Giving CPR to an Adult

__a__ **13.** Look inside the victim's mouth. If you see anything blocking the airway, remove it.

_____ **14.** Check for signs of circulation, such as breathing, coughing, or movement. If there are no signs of circulation, a person trained in CPR should begin chest compressions immediately.

_____ **15.** Lay the person flat on a firm surface.

_____ **16.** If victim is not breathing, begin rescue breathing.

Applying Health Skills

Refusal Skills

Staying Safe

With a partner, create a role-play about a teen who uses refusal skills to avoid unsafe behavior.

1. With your partner, choose a situation in which a teen is pressured to do something unsafe. Choose one of the situations in the boxes below, and put a check mark in that box. If you prefer, make up your own situation. Write a brief description of that situation in the empty box.

> Miguel has offered to teach Olivia how to skateboard. He says that she can borrow his sister's helmet and knee and elbow pads. When Olivia gets to Miguel's house, however, she finds that Miguel's sister has loaned her equipment to someone else.

> Sasha and Jasmine have made plans to go hiking together in a national forest. However, the weather report is now predicting thunderstorms and hail for the day of their hike. Jasmine does not think it's safe for them to be outside and far from home in bad weather like that.

> Daniel invites Yoni to go swimming in a section of the lake that has "No Swimming" signs posted. Yoni knows that this part of the lake is known for its sudden drop offs and rocky bottom.

> _____
> _____
> _____
> _____
> _____

2. With your partner, discuss how one teen in the role-play will pressure the other. Also, discuss how the other teen will use refusal skills to avoid the unsafe behavior.

3. Together, practice role-playing the situation. Then present your role-play to the rest of the class.

Chapter 21 Study Guide
Environmental Health

Study Tips
✔ Read the chapter objectives.
✔ Look up any unfamiliar words.
✔ Read the questions below before you read the chapter.

As you read the chapter, answer the following questions. Later you can use this guide to review the information in the chapter.

Lesson 1

1. What are some of the major sources of air pollution?

_____

_____

_____

_____

_____

2. What are pesticides?

_____

_____

_____

3. What are some of the effects of air pollution?

_____

_____

_____

_____

4. What is smog?

_____

_____

_____

_____

Chapter 21 Study Guide
Environmental Health

5. What is the ozone layer?

_____

_____

_____

6. What are hazardous wastes? Name some examples of hazardous wastes.

_____

_____

_____

_____

_____

_____

Lesson 2

7. What is the Environmental Protection Agency?

_____

_____

_____

8. What are some ways you can help to keep the air clean?

_____

_____

_____

_____

_____

_____

9. What are nonrenewable resources?

_____

_____

Chapter 21

Chapter 21 Study Guide
Environmental Health

10. What is conservation?

_____

_____

11. What does biodegradable mean?

_____

_____

12. What is precycling, and how can you do this?

_____

_____

_____

_____

_____

_____

Chapter 21

Activity 89
Use with Chapter 21, Lesson 1

Pollution and Health

Imagine that you are on a quiz show. One of the categories is pollution. The quiz show host presents an answer. You must supply the question.

1. Answer: Results from ongoing human activities that release gases, dust, soot, and other substances into the air.

Question: _____

2. Answer: Burning this releases toxic gases that harm the atmosphere.

Question: _____

3. Answer: Any dirty or harmful substances in the environment.

Question: _____

4. Answer: A yellow-brown haze that forms when sunlight reacts with air pollution.

Question: _____

5. Answer: 4.4 pounds.

Question: _____

6. Answer: Used on crops to control insects and other pests.

Question: _____

7. Answer: Air pollution intensifies this.

Question: _____

8. Answer: Acts as a shield that protects living things from ultraviolet (UV) radiation.

Question: _____

9. Answer: A rise in the earth's temperatures.

Question: _____

10. Answer: Human-made liquid or solid wastes that may endanger human health or the environment.

Question: _____

Chapter 21

Activity 90
Use with Chapter 21, Lesson 2

Preventing and Reducing Pollution

Suggest a way to reduce, reuse, or recycle each waste item listed below. Then answer the question that follows. One item has been filled in as an example.

	Plastic Grocery Bag	Glass Pickle Jar	Used White Computer Paper	Out of Fashion Jeans
Reduce			Print only when it is necessary.	
Reuse			Use both sides of the paper.	
Recycle			Use as scratch paper for notes.	

What products do you think are worst for the environment? Explain your answer.

_____

_____

_____

_____

_____

_____

Chapter 21 Health Inventory

How Do You Help the Environment?

Rate your awareness of environmental problems and what you can do to help. For each item below, circle the word that tells how often you behave as described.

Always   Sometimes   Never   **1.** I use reusable materials instead of paper plates and cups.

Always   Sometimes   Never   **2.** I buy in bulk when I can.

Always   Sometimes   Never   **3.** Rather than ride in the car, I walk or ride my bike when I can.

Always   Sometimes   Never   **4.** I use public transportation whenever necessary.

Always   Sometimes   Never   **5.** I turn off radios and TVs when I am not using them.

Always   Sometimes   Never   **6.** I turn down the heat when no one is home.

Always   Sometimes   Never   **7.** I help recycle paper, plastic, aluminum, and glass.

Always   Sometimes   Never   **8.** I do not run the dishwasher or washing machine unless I have a full load.

Always   Sometimes   Never   **9.** I take a reusable plastic bag with me when I shop to hold my purchases.

Always   Sometimes   Never   **10.** I do not leave water running.

Always   Sometimes   Never   **11.** I choose products that are packaged in reusable or recycled packaging.

Always   Sometimes   Never   **12.** I reuse items by repairing them, selling them, or donating them to charity.

Always   Sometimes   Never   **13.** I am willing to volunteer my time to make the environment cleaner and safer.

Always   Sometimes   Never   **14.** I use biodegradable detergents and other products.

Score yourself:

Give yourself three points for each *Always* answer, 1 point for each *Sometimes* answer, and 0 for each *never* answer. Write your score here.

36–42: Excellent! You are doing your part for a healthy environment.

26–35: Good. You are trying. Keep up the effort.

Fewer than 26: You need to do a better job of protecting the environment. See what you can do to improve. This is the only world we get.

Chapter 21

NOTES

NOTES

NOTES

NOTES